IELTS

雅思口语

全攻略 冲刺篇

毕绪强 编著

U0139422

北京语言大学出版社
BEIJING LANGUAGE AND CULTURE
UNIVERSITY PRESS

© 2022 北京语言大学出版社，社图号 21170

图书在版编目（CIP）数据

雅思口语全攻略．冲刺篇 ／ 毕绪强编著．－－ 北京 ：
北京语言大学出版社，2022.6
ISBN 978-7-5619-5994-7

Ⅰ.①雅…　Ⅱ.①毕…　Ⅲ.① IELTS －口语－自学参
考资料　Ⅳ.①H319.9

中国版本图书馆 CIP 数据核字 (2021) 第 202624 号

雅思口语全攻略：冲刺篇
YASI KOUYU QUAN GONGLÜE: CHONGCI PIAN

责任编辑：孙冠群
排版制作：北京创艺涵文化发展有限公司
责任印制：周　燚

出版发行：北京语言大学出版社
社　　址：北京市海淀区学院路 15 号，100083
网　　址：www.blcup.com
电子信箱：service@blcup.com
电　　话：编 辑 部　8610-82301019
　　　　　国内发行　8610-82303650/3591/3648
　　　　　海外发行　8610-82303365/3080/3668
　　　　　北语书店　8610-82303653
　　　　　网购咨询　8610-82303908
印　　刷：北京中科印刷有限公司

版　　次：2022 年 6 月第 1 版　　印　　次：2022 年 6 月第 1 次印刷
开　　本：787 毫米 × 1092 毫米　1/16　　印　　张：12.25
字　　数：272 千字
定　　价：59.00 元

PRINTED IN CHINA
凡有印装质量问题，本社负责调换。售后 QQ：1367565611，电话：010–82303590

序

在雅思考试中，口语部分是较难得到满分的一个考试单项。很多考生通过背诵口语答案备考。而在实际考试时，如果考生的回答被考官认定是背诵的，那么其口语成绩一般不会超过5.5分。有些考生无论如何努力练习、背诵，口语成绩都维持在5.5分左右；有些基础不错的考生在系统的培训和老师的指导、陪练下也总是无法突破口语6.5分的瓶颈。这大多与考生平时积累较少有关。多数考生在口语素材积累、观点组织、语言表达、发音和流利度等方面确实存在欠缺和不足。尽管有时考生在考场上自我感觉发挥得不错，回答流利，思路顺畅，互动回应良好，但是实际上他们的语言质量还是非常课本化的，不够地道、学术，没有达到相应评分标准的要求。

雅思口语三个部分的考题各有其侧重考查的能力。第一部分（Part 1）为基本信息问答，考查考生基本交流和个人思想表达的能力。由于考官会预设性地认为考生都是在培训机构学过模板、参考过"机经"、背过答案的，为了检测考生的真实语言水平，考官会通过不断地转换话题来测评考生是否在背答案。从购物到运动、从旅行到个人喜好，考生必须在回答每类问题时都保持稳定的答题状态、流畅度和语言质量。第二部分（Part 2）会有题库话题的题卡（cue card），主要是四大类话题：人物、物品、事件、地点。为了防止考生背答案、按照模板套路答题，题目出法已经变得越来越细，也就是说，考题会在话题的核心概念上添加多层限定。例如，人物类题目中要求考生描述一位老师："Describe a math teacher in primary school who helped you a lot."这里就需要注意其限定条件：math、in primary school、helped you a lot。准备时间为1分钟，考生可以用白板和记号笔做笔记。答题时间为1~2分钟，时间到了考官会告诉考生停止答题。在回答第二部分的题目时，考生需要对具体的时间、地点、参与的人物、事件经过、意义与感受等进行详细描述，展现自己的叙述能力、逻辑能力以及总结和评论能力。第三部分（Part 3）的题目为第二部分话题的延伸，主要是针对与第二部分相关的延伸话题进行评述，例如，比较过去与现在的区别、预测某种趋势走向、分析老年人与青年人对某个问题的不同态度和做法等。考生在回答时要客观地、有逻辑地讲出自己的见解和观点，注意一定要避免"空""大""泛"的问题。

对于雅思口语考试来说，获取高分的基础在于考生回答的内容质量要高，要让考官觉得考生回答的内容、前后逻辑、语法、词汇、语音语调等都没有问题，找不到任何可以扣分的点。考生在考场上要有良好的答题状态，语言要流畅、有逻辑，语音语调有节奏感，让自己处于放松的状态才能让考官也感觉到轻松和惬意，这样容易提高考官对考生语言使用的能力评级。下面提供一个口语得分参考表格，考生在平时练习时可以按照这个表格来评定自己的口语回答。

回 应	5.5	6.0	6.5	7.0	7.5	8	8.5	9
主题								
逻辑								
举例								
信息效率								
语言质量								
地道短句								
学术句型								
句间衔接								
语法多样性								
词汇丰富性								
发音								
节奏								
流畅度								
音量								

很多考生比较担心雅思考试的换题季，要尽量赶在换题前完成考试，以免无法应对雅思口语的新题。实际上，口语题目基本上只会换掉一部分，而考生面对的真正的问题是恒定不变的，那就是自己实际的英语水平。无论面对的是新题还是老题，考生只有全面提高自己的英语水平，多学多练多积累，才能以不变应万变。对于"机经"题库，建议考生进行分类整理，并进行整体有序的练习，积累实战经验，逐渐提高自己的答题效率和水平。不建议考生在网上购买所谓的押题和预测，其中的题目和答案的质量是不高的。

备考雅思口语，不能靠盲目背诵答案，而是应该在熟悉各类题目话题的基础上，积累观点、素材、例子、句型、词汇和表达等，并通过大量的日常练习，锻炼口语流利度和发音。本书将近年来常考的雅思口语话题细致分类，提供各类话题的高分回答，为考生提供答题思路参考。书中还汇总了地道的英语口语表达句式和词汇，有助于考生积累、拓展口语语料。针对口语考试的三个部分，提供实用的考场流程信息和冲刺备考攻略。此外，本书还汇总了雅思口语高频句型和常用句法，帮助考生集中学习。

祝各位考生都能顺利通过考试，取得理想分数！

毕绪强

目 录

V

第 一 章

Part 1 冲刺技巧

IELTS

SPEAKING

一、考场流程与良好的第一印象

雅思口语考试为"与考官一对一进行口语交流"的口语测评考试。纸笔考试的口语考试通常会安排在笔试前一周至笔试后一周的任意一天，机考的口语考试通常会安排在笔试当天或者与笔试日期尽可能相邻的日期。考生应提前40~50分钟到考场外等待，大约提前30分钟入场。考生须携带与报名时完全一致的有效身份证件原件，并参加现场照相和指纹采集。参加纸笔考试的考生要注意，所有考生统一进入考场区后需要在各考试教室外等候考官出来叫考生进入考试教室。在前一位考生考完走出来之后，其他考生要继续在门外候考而不要直接进去，更不要敲门，因为考官可能还没有评完分数，不希望被打扰。

进入考场后，考官会说"Please take a seat."，此时考生可回答"Thank you, sir/madam."，然后考官与考生面对面坐下，考官开始进行程序化录音，内容包括讲明本次考试的日期、考区、考场、考官号码及姓名、考生号码及姓名。然后考官会问一些开场问题，比如"Can you tell me your full name, please?"，并正式开始考试。在 Part 1，考官一般会提问与考生个人情况相关的问题，比如"Are you a student?""What do you do?"。在回答第一个问题时，考生就要开始对答案进行设计，因为考官会根据具体的回答开始判定相应的分数段。注意，考生的回答一定要有自己的观点，并且自然流畅，这样可以给考官留下良好的印象。每个问题建议回答15~20秒。答题时注意节奏、语调，一定不要给考官留下在"背答案"的印象，组织答案时最好使用更多地道的短句，而非长且复杂的句子。

二、和考官聊出"对的感觉"来

雅思口语考试 Part 1 的问题大多与考生的基本信息相关，考查考生的英文交流和表达能力，话题涉及购物、运动、旅行、个人喜好等。考生在答题时，要抓住题目核心词及其限定条件，有针对性地进行回应。首先，语言要有信息效率，剔除一切无效、低效语言和各类铺垫以及重复性内容。合理运用指示代词，减少用词的重复，同时还要避免"空""大""泛"。另外，要注意语言质量。雅思口语考试测评的主要是语言水平，考生要在回答问题的过程中，向考官展示自己的语言能力。考生的回答首先要保证语法正确、用词准确，在此基础上通过变换不同的句型句式、使用丰富多样的词汇和地道的习语来让自己的回答脱颖而出，给考官留下良好印象。

需要提醒考生的是，在词汇方面，用词要正确、恰当，合理搭配，不需要全部使用难词、生僻词等来体现自己的词汇量。在发音方面，只要做到发音清晰、准确即可。地道、标准的英式或美式发音确实会为考生的回答增色、加分，但这需要长期的大量练习。考生在答题时应更加注意互动感和交流感，让考官对你的回答有所感触、有所共鸣是比较理想的。

三、误区和雷区

1. 痴迷考前预测

英语口语基础薄弱的考生以及备考时间比较短的考生，在考试之前会比较倾向于偏信一些考前预测或押题，从而缩小备考题目范围。这么做一方面会导致考生准备的话题类型不全面，不利于备考；另一方面，考生如果在考场上没有被问到考前预测的题目，很可能会产生挫败感，影响现场发挥。即使考前预测的题目在考试中遇到了，如果只是背诵准备好的答案，也不会得高分。考官很容易能听出考生是否在生搬硬背事先备好的答案，毕竟考官是整体接触大量样本考生的"老江湖"了。与其临阵磨枪押题，不如逐一选取各分类话题中有代表性的题目进行研读和练习，举一反三，吸收其中的高分句型和地道表达，以此为基础在考场上进行自由拆分和组合，让能力的提升带动分数的提高。

2. 流利就是高分

有些考生刻意追求语言表达的流利和语速的提高，而在语言质量和信息效率方面毫无进步。如果考生在语、句、词方面表现一般，且常伴随低级错误和中式思维，那么再流利的语言也不会赢来高分，特别是当流利的语言中并未给出有效的信息的时候。打好语言基础、把握题目关键并精准回应、培养逻辑思维和表达能力，都是考生层层修炼终得正果的必经之路。因此，长期、踏实的练习是至关重要的。

3. 说得多就能得高分

有些考生虽然平时能和一些外教聊得不错，面对考官时也能口若悬河，但如果考生没有精准理解题目要点，没有进行"直接有效的回应"，答非所问，那么说得再多都不会得高分。除此之外，考生还需要在学术话题和词汇方面做更多储备，让自己不管面对什么问题都能回答得有理有据，言之有物。

4. 语速平、没表情

有些考生在考场上可能会过度紧张，回答问题时声音过小，语调平淡，没有节奏与互动。虽然雅思口语考试不要求考生在考场上声情并茂地进行演讲，但考生最好能让考官在你的回答中感受到真情实感的自然流露，而非只是在应付一道口语题。

5. 过于在乎考官的反应

有些考生在看到考官全程面无表情或时而皱眉时，答题情绪和状态会颇受影响。其实考官各有不同，有的非常和善、周到，会在交流中与考生互动或给予鼓励、肯定的眼神并耐心聆听，有的则对考生的态度比较冷漠。但是，无论考官有着怎样的表情和态度，他们都会客观地对考生进行评测并给出符合考生实际英语水平的分数。因此，在口语考试中，不要过于在意考官的反应，应该集中精力答好每一道题。

6. 同质化的口语练习

有些考生基本不练习或者很少练习口语，他们认为应在临考前再练习，因为他们觉得练习过早容易忘，或者没有老师的指导和陪伴就没有办法练习口语。即使考生会练习，他们大多也会在同一水平区间进行循环反复的练习，而很少进行深度练习。笔者建议考生按照"测、练、改、比、学、背、用"的循环闭环来练习口语。具体该怎么做呢？针对一道口语题，考生首先自己进行测试性练习，可以准备多个版本的回答，答题的同时录音，然后回放录音，逐句精听，将自己的口语答案优化润色。接下来就是找到针对相同题目的优质范文，与自己的回答进行比较，学习其答题思路，吸收其中高质量的句型、语料、观点和素材，对自己的答案进一步润色。之后把优质范文背下来并消化吸收，再通过练习类似的题目把所学的语、句、词进行自由拆分组合，举一反三，重新组织答案。通过这样的循环练习，不断积累，才能从根本上提高口语实力，在考场上不管遇到什么题目，都能迅速反应，给出逻辑清晰、有理有据的高分回答。

Part 1 机经话题分类实战

IELTS

SPEAKING

第一节　地点类 Places

1. Countryside

(1) Would you like to live in the countryside in the future?

Yes, of course. I can always feel relaxed in the countryside, because I can get a chance to enjoy a lot of things that I could ever want, such as a private garden, several pets, a peaceful lifestyle, and simple interpersonal relationships that I always desire. With fresher air and cleaner water, I could lead a healthier life there.

亮点句型

- I can get a chance to enjoy a lot of things that I could ever want.

地道表达

- private garden　私家花园
- peaceful lifestyle　宁静的生活方式
- healthier life　更健康的生活

(2) What do the people who live in the countryside like to do?

Many people living in the countryside have their own gardens or small farms, getting away from the noise of the city. They can grow some vegetables with organic fertiliser, and enjoy their pleasant pastoral life. They also like to take part in some outdoor activities, such as picking fruits in the wild or fishing by the lake.

地道表达

- organic fertiliser　有机肥料
- pastoral life　田园生活

(3) What are the benefits of living in the countryside?

People are keen on rural idyllic life, because in the countryside people can escape from the noise of the metropolis. Thanks to the slower-paced life in the countryside, people can acquire inner peace, immerse themselves in the unspoiled natural environment, and relieve stress and anxiety. Besides, it is easier to get fresh vegetables and fruits in the countryside, which is also beneficial to people's health.

地道表达

- be keen on sth.　对某事有兴趣
- rural idyllic life　乡村田园诗般的生活
- the noise of the metropolis　城市的喧嚣
- thanks to...　多亏了……

- immerse in...　沉浸于……
- relieve stress and anxiety　缓解压力和焦虑

(4) What's the difference between living in the city and living in the countryside?

Well, the differences are huge and obvious. City life means convenience, with numerous 24-hour chain stores, plenty of educational resources, comprehensive sanitation facilities, and huge amounts of job opportunities. However, although people living in the countryside have to handle everything mostly by themselves, like the house maintenance or renovation, the rural life is quieter and more relaxing.

地道表达

- plenty of educational resources　很多教育资源
- sanitation facilities　卫生设备

- handle　应对
- house maintenance or renovation　房屋维修或翻新

2. Hometown

(1) What's the name of your hometown? Please describe your hometown.

My hometown is Jinan, which is famous for the plenty of natural springs there. It is a city both ancient and modern, with thousands of years' culture woven into the urban tapestry. There are millions of friendly people in this city who would welcome people from the world with unrestrained enthusiasm. Having said that though, I wish the air there could be as clean as that of Qingdao and the traffic not that congested all the time.

地道表达

- a city both ancient and modern　既古老又现代的城市
- with thousands of years' culture woven

- into...　伴随着数千年的文化交织进……
- as clean as that of...　如……的那样干净

(2) Do you like your hometown? Do you like living there?

Yes, I do. Even though I have always been complaining about the haze lasting for almost half a year and the traffic congestion during peak hours, it is still a pleasant place to live in, with a relatively slow-paced lifestyle and amicable working environments, as well as friendly local people.

地道表达

- complain about... 抱怨……
- traffic congestion 交通堵塞
- slow-paced lifestyle 慢节奏的生活方式
- amicable working environment 友好的工作环境

(3) What do you like most about your hometown?

What I particularly like about it is that there are millions of friendly people living in this city, making it one of the most welcoming places in China. It is also one of the safest cities in China, with a very low crime rate, and thus I could walk alone in the late night without worrying about safety problems. People there go the extra mile to help you when you are in need, earning the city a reputation for its friendliness, which is also something I am always proud of.

亮点句型

- What I particularly like about it is that...

地道表达

- crime rate 犯罪率
- earn a reputation 赢得声誉
- be proud of... 因……而自豪

(4) Is there anything you dislike about it?

My hometown is a medium-sized inland city, where ambitious young people may find it hard to have suitable jobs. If they want to work in the world-famous Fortune 500 companies, they have to relocate to metropolises like Beijing and Shanghai. Another point I have to say is that the air pollution in the city has been severe, and immediate action should be taken.

亮点句型

- Another point I have to say is that...

地道表达

- medium-sized inland city 中等内陆城市
- relocate to... 移居到……

3. Living places

(1) Can you describe the community in which you live?

I live in a community in the downtown area, where there are many bus stops nearby. There is also an open park, just five minutes' walk away. Just one stop to the west is the primary school I once attended. Something worth mentioning is that a Starbucks, my favourite café, is also within walking distance. So the place I live in is quite convenient for office workers like me.

亮点句型

- I live in...area, where...
- Something worth mentioning is that...

地道表达

- downtown area　市中心
- bus stop　公交车站
- primary school　小学
- within walking distance　在步行可达的距离内
- office worker　上班族

(2) What do you do in your bedroom?

The bedroom is the best place to have quality sleep at night, because I am always busy and tired in the daytime. Besides, other than sleeping, I stay in my bedroom reading books or browsing websites to search for the information I want during my spare time, accompanied by my pet dog. Sometimes, I do yoga for an hour, getting into a state of meditation in my bedroom.

地道表达

- quality sleep　优质睡眠
- busy and tired　又忙又累

(3) What kind of decorations does it have?

My bedroom is decorated in a modern Mediterranean style, with simple and elegant design. Like most Westerners, I put up a lot of family photos on the walls as decorations. There is also a small display cabinet to show my souvenirs that I brought back from many other countries. These are the ways in which I decorate my bedroom.

地道表达

- simple and elegant　简单而优雅
- display cabinet　陈列柜
- souvenir　纪念品

(4) How well do you know your neighbours?

Actually, we barely know each other, although we live next door on the same floor. We seldom meet each other，so I guess maybe we have quite different schedules. And this is a common scene in China where most people are busy focusing on their own things. Most of us simply say hello and nod to greet our neighbours, without wasting any effort in getting to know our neighbours just a bit more.

地道表达

- focus on...　关注……
- waste sth. (in) doing sth.　浪费，滥用

(5) Would you say that the place you live in is good for families with children?

Well, I should say yes. There is a well-equipped kindergarten in our community. Parents could leave their children there in the daytime, and the professional staff will take good care of their children. There are also a primary school and a middle school, which can help solve the problem of where children can go to school.

地道表达

- well-equipped　设施齐全的
- take care of...　照顾……

4. Museums

(1) Are there many museums in your hometown?

Well, there are a lot of museums in my hometown, since it is a capital city full of culture and history. We have an Art Museum, a Science and Technology Museum, a History Museum, etc., which are all funded by the local government. These museums are established to preserve the historical and cultural treasures and provide a window for citizens and tourists to understand the history of the city and appreciate its brilliance.

地道表达

- preserve the historical and cultural treasures　保存历史和文化的瑰宝

(2) Do you often visit a museum?

I used to visit museums regularly when I was a student, because these activities were regularly organised by our schools. I am now out of college, so I just visit the local museums occasionally whenever my friends from different cultural backgrounds need my company. However, when I travel to other places, I often pay visits to the local museums.

- used to do sth. 过去常常做某事
- be regularly organised 被经常组织

(3) Do you think it's suitable for museums to sell things to visitors?

I think it is acceptable. It will increase the revenue of the museums, and thus the museums could have more funds to better preserve the collections they have, alleviating the financial burden on the government. For the visitors, they could buy some souvenirs sold in the museums as a memento of the good time they had visiting the museum.

地道表达

- increase the revenue of... 增加……的收入
- financial burden 财政负担

5. Public places

(1) Are there many public places in your country?

Well, there are plenty of public places in my country. Some are free of charge. For example, city squares, municipal libraries, river esplanade parks, and so on. Some of the public places may charge for admission, such as the botanical gardens, city zoos and museums.

地道表达

- free of charge 免费的
- municipal library 市图书馆
- river esplanade park 河滨公园
- charge for admission 收入场费
- botanical garden 植物园

(2) Are public gardens very important in China?

Yes, of course. For people who live in the cement forests in the urban area, public gardens of various sizes where people can relax and enjoy fresh air are essential. The public gardens offer people a nice respite and help them forget of chores at home or the hustle and bustle of life temporally, especially in metropolises like Shanghai and Beijing.

地道表达

- of various sizes 不同规模的
- offer people a nice respite 为人们提供一个好的喘息机会

(3) Are there many public gardens in your country?

No, there aren't. The more developed the city is, the fewer public gardens there are. They have always been overlooked in my country, as the city planning departments always prioritise the land for industrial purposes such as downtown buildings, city complexes, and residential communities. Undoubtedly, little land would be left for gardens, which is a pity I should say.

亮点句型
- ...have always been overlooked...

地道表达
- city planning　城市规划
- residential communities　居民区

(4) Do you think there are enough public gardens in your hometown?

I should say that the number is far from enough. There is merely one botanical garden in my hometown, and here in the urban area, we do not have any other open gardens. The only places in which people can embrace nature and get a nice shade are the meagre green spaces in their community compounds.

地道表达
- far from enough　远远不够
- get a nice shade　享受阴凉
- meagre　少且劣质的
- green spaces　绿色空间，绿地

(5) Do you like doing exercise in public places, such as parks?

I should say no. I am a homebody and I enjoy exercising at home. It is much cozier at home because I can regulate the room temperature through air conditioning. I enjoy the quietness so that I can easily meditate while practising yoga. When I exercise on the running machine, I could even watch TV at the same time, which is kind of relaxing. Each time after exercising, I can have a bath immediately and go back to work.

地道表达
- homebody　喜欢待在家里的人
- running machine　跑步机

6. Schools

(1) How old were you when you started schooling?

I began primary school at the age of 6, one year younger than most of my classmates. I was keen to go to school with my friends from the neighbourhood at the time and I hoped to attend the same grade with them. Though there is an age gap between my friends and me, I still built a strong relationship with them.

地道表达

- be keen to do sth. 渴望做某事
- at the time 当时

(2) How did you get to school every day?

When I was a primary school student, my parents always drove me to school out of safety concerns. I started walking to school with my friends when I was a middle school student, because the school I attended was just a few minutes' walk away. Occasionally, I went to school by bicycle in spring and autumn, enjoying the pleasant breeze.

地道表达

- out of safety concerns 出于安全考虑
- occasionally 偶尔
- a few minutes' walk away 步行几分钟的路

(3) Tell me something about the school you attended.

The high school I attended ranked top five for its academic performance and its average score for the SATs. We had many superb school facilities, like an auditorium that could house 500 students for lectures, an indoor stadium with great sports equipment, as well as a mini botanical garden.

地道表达

- house 500 students 容纳 500 个学生
- indoor stadium 室内体育场

Notes

第二节　生活类 Life experiences

1. Advertisements

(1) Why do you think there are so many advertisements?

Actually, the choices of products with similar functions greatly exceed the actual needs of buyers, which means that the competition between different brands is incredibly fierce. In order to make their products stand out and attract buyers, manufacturers have to increase the exposure rate of their products. Thus, tons of ads are made and shown repetitively to impress upon potential buyers. In short, advertising is used to promote sales.

地道表达
- with similar functions　具有相似功能的
- the actual needs of buyers　购买者的实际需要
- incredibly fierce　极其激烈
- stand out　突出，引人注目
- increase the exposure rate　增加曝光率
- potential buyer　潜在买家
- in short　总之

(2) What are the places where we see advertisements?

Well, advertisements are actually everywhere. We can find them on TV, newspapers, billboards, flyers, trade stands, and even on buses. At present, advertisements take various forms. For example, there are ads painted on buses, flyers stuck up in stairwells, and posters hung in lifts. We can also see advertisements on our mobile phones when using various apps.

地道表达
- billboard　广告展板
- flyer　宣传单页
- trade stand　柜台
- ad　广告
- poster　海报

(3) How do you feel about advertisements?

Well, I have a high opinion of good advertisements that can clearly demonstrate the core features and main selling points of products. Such ads can tell me why a certain product could be the better choice. Besides, some well-made advertisements are full of creativity, amusing us as if we are watching short films.

- high opinion　好评
- as if　好像……一样
- selling point　卖点

(4) Do advertisements influence your choice about what to buy?

Yes, they do. I am often convinced that the quality and the taste of a product must be good if the product is recommended by a celebrity I like. In many cases, I'm attracted to the fantastic presentation of the new products in the ads. Those ads often persuade me to buy things I do not need at the time.

地道表达

- be convinced that...　坚信……
- in many cases　在很多情况下
- celebrity　名人
- presentation　展示

2. Being alone

(1) What do you like to do when you are alone?

It depends primarily on what I am in the mood for. Usually, I read books, especially those classics, some of which are best sellers, such as *Pride and Prejudice*, and so on. Occasionally I take a walk, watch films or go shopping by myself.

亮点句型

- It depends primarily on...

地道表达

- in the mood for...　有心情做……
- best seller　畅销书

(2) Do you wish to have more time alone?

Yes, I do. I always feel good to be alone, because it means I am totally in charge of my time. When I'm alone, I can indulge myself in my own world, and fully relax while reading novels or watching movies. It helps me to find inner peace in my busy life.

地道表达

- in charge of...　负责……，掌管……

3. Being in a hurry

(1) When was the last time you did something in a hurry?

Well, it was a Saturday morning last month, when I almost missed a train. I found out I had mixed up the departure time, so I ran out of my home and took a taxi. I had to make a detour to avoid traffic jams and the car took a speedup at full speed to reach the train platform in the last few minutes. Fortunately, I caught the train just before the door closed.

地道表达

- the departure time 出发时间
- make a detour 绕行

(2) Do you like to finish things quickly?

I pride myself on my high efficiency, and I like to have jobs finished as soon as possible. Although it is a little bit tiring at first, I never need to worry about deadlines.

地道表达

- high efficiency 高效率
- worry about deadlines 担心截止日期

(3) What kinds of things will you never do in a hurry?

I will never make decisions in haste. When I have to make important decisions, I usually turn to my family, relatives, and friends for advice. As the old proverb goes, 'Haste makes waste.' It is risky to make a quick decision without taking everything into account and carefully balancing pros and cons.

亮点句型

- It is risky to make a quick decision without...

地道表达

- turn to... 求助于……
- take...into account 考虑到……
- Haste makes waste 欲速则不达
- pros and cons 优缺点

(4) Why do people make mistakes more easily when they are in a hurry?

People are prone to make mistakes in a hurry, because they will take action before thinking carefully. When people act in haste, it is hard for them to keep calm and stay reasonable as usual. They may lose their clear judgement, which often leads to bad consequences.

地道表达

- be prone to do... 容易做……
- take action 采取行动
- lead to 导致

4. Clothes

(1) Do you think people would like to spend a great amount of money on clothing?

It varies with age, gender, occupation and social status. Young ladies may spend half of their income on clothing to catch up with new fashion. Some business people spend a huge amount of money on tailor-made fine clothes, while the elderly tend to wear the same old clothes for years to save money.

地道表达

- vary with... 根据……而不同
- tailor-made fine clothes 量身定做的好衣服

(2) What kind of clothes do you like to wear?

Casual wear has always been my favorite, like jeans, T-shirts, something that I can mix and match at will. For some formal occasions, I prefer to wear nice and formal suits, which make me look neat and smart.

地道表达

- at will 随心地，按个人意愿

5. Photos

(1) Do you prefer paper photos or electronic photos?

I personally prefer electronic photos because I can store them on my mobile phone and view them at any time. I could also edit the photos on my phone, adding words, adjusting colours, things like that. By comparison, paper photos are not so convenient and may fade over the years. Thus, e-photos are much better.

地道表达

- edit 编辑
- by comparison 相比较而言
- fade over the years 随着岁月的流逝而褪色

(2) Do you have a professional camera?

Well, I am not a good photographer, and I do not have any professional camera. However, I can take a lot of good pictures thanks to the apps on my mobile phone. Honestly speaking, with these apps, people could take pictures that are even better than the ones taken with professional cameras, especially by those phones specially designed for photo taking.

地道表达

- honestly speaking   老实说
- phones specially designed for photo taking   专门为拍照设计的手机

(3) Do you think photos are important?

Well, actually, I believe photos are useful and important. As to the photos on credentials, such as passport photos, ID photos, etc., they help people prove their identities. As to the photos of scenery and products, they convey important information to people as a form of reference. Finally, as to the photos taken at some important life moments, they could help preserve good memories for the people who keep them.

地道表达

- credential   证件
- prove identities   证明身份
- convey important information   传递重要的信息
- important life moments   人生的重大时刻
- preserve   保存

(4) Do you think high quality photos come from expensive cameras?

No, I don't think so. I admit that good cameras are usually equipped with more advanced optical sensors, which could capture the light better and make the colours depicted in the photos more vivid and more natural. However, I believe that the scenes captured in the photos, the composition of the pictures, as well as the precious memories kept in the photos are all more important.

地道表达

- be equipped with...   配备······
- optical sensor   光学传感器
- capture the light   捕捉光线
- more vivid   更加鲜活
- the composition of the pictures   构图

(5) When you visit other places, do you take photos or buy postcards?

Of course I will take photos. As an amateur photographer, I always take good quality pictures, depicting swimming fish, flying birds, the sunrise or the sunset, things like that. I can make the photos into e-postcards and then send them to my friends. I think it is much more meaningful than sending postcards bought at gift shops.

地道表达

- as an amateur photographer 作为一名
  业余摄影爱好者
- good quality pictures 高质量的图片
- the sunrise or the sunset 日出或者日落

6. Public holidays

(1) What public holidays do you have in your country?

Well, there are a lot of public holidays in my country. We have the May Day holiday, the National Day holiday and traditional holidays such as the Tomb Sweeping Day, the Dragon Boat Festival, the Mid-Autumn Festival, as well as the most important one for all Chinese, the Spring Festival.

地道表达

- May Day 五一劳动节
- National Day 国庆节
- the Tomb Sweeping Day 清明节
- the Dragon Boat Festival 端午节
- the Mid-Autumn Festival 中秋节
- the Spring Festival 春节

(2) What do people in your country usually do on public holidays?

Since many people do not have much time for long journeys at ordinary times, they tend to spend most of their vacations travelling. As a result, during public holidays, almost all the scenic spots are crowded with people. Some people choose to stay at home and relax on public holidays.

地道表达

- at ordinary times 平时
- scenic spot 景区

(3) Do you like public holidays?

Yes, I do. During these holidays, I usually have days off, so I can indulge myself in activities that I don't have time to do on weekdays, like having a sleepover at a friend's house, trying out new food outlets, visiting museums, or just watching TV at home.

- have days off 休息几天
- have a sleepover 在外过夜，聚会

(4) What did you do during the last public holiday?

I did something special during my last public holiday, the seven day-off National Day. I cut off all contact with other people, turned off my phone, disconnected the network, and just stayed at home alone. I did some laundry, cleaned the house, and read several books. Without the anxiety of responding to tons of emails and messages, I felt happy and relaxed during this holiday.

地道表达

- turn off one's phone 关闭手机
- disconnect the network 切断网络

7. Sleeping

(1) How many hours do you sleep every day?

About 7 hours I should say. I usually go to bed at 11 pm and get up at 6 am. I always keep to a regular timetable of sleeping and waking, and each morning when I wake up, I feel full of energy. I never compromise the quality of my sleep, especially after I watched a TED talk about sleeping, which tells the importance of a sound sleep with reliable research results.

地道表达

- keep to 坚持，履行
- full of energy 充满活力
- a sound sleep 酣睡
- reliable 可靠的

(2) Is it necessary to sleep enough?

It is essential to get adequate sleep, as it not only helps the body get sufficient rest but also makes us feel energetic. I don't think it is a good idea to sacrifice sleep for extra study time in the long run. All work and no play makes Jack a dull boy.

亮点句型

- I don't think it is a good idea to...

地道表达

- in the long run 从长远来看
- all work and no play makes Jack a dull boy 只工作不休息，聪明孩子也变傻

(3) Is taking a nap important?

It depends. It is just a matter of personal habit. To those who are not used to having a nap, they are still energetic even if they don't get some sleep after lunch. But to those who make it a part of their daily routine, they may feel extremely tired and sleepy in the afternoon if they don't get the nap they need.

地道表达

- a matter of personal habit 个人习惯问题
- a part of one's daily routine 某人日常生活的一部分

(4) Do you stay up late quite often?

Well, sometimes. Especially when exams are imminent, I have to burn the midnight oil to study, or sometimes I stay up nights for the thesis that I have to complete. After that, I can go back to my regular life, and go to bed much earlier.

地道表达

- imminent 临近的
- burn the midnight oil 开夜车，睡得晚

8. Sounds and noise

(1) What sounds do you like?

I like the sound of nature, the harmony composed by insects, birds, rivers and mountains. They are the most beautiful sounds, though I seldom hear them in the city. I also like the sound of rain, especially the sound made by rain pattering on the roof. This sound can always help me find inner peace and fall asleep easily.

地道表达

- the sound of nature 自然的声音

(2) Do you think there is more noise in people's lives today than in the past?

Well, yes, definitely. Noise is one of the problems of modern society. Noise is everywhere. Factories, machines, electrical appliances, and cars etc. are all sources of noise. People in the past lived a much quieter life.

地道表达

- electrical appliances 电器

9. Weekends

(1) How do you usually spend your weekends?

I do have a pretty regular schedule on weekends. On Saturday mornings, I usually get up whenever I want to, so that I can get enough sleep and recharge. In the afternoons, I often play tennis with some friends and we party together afterwards. I try to keep Sundays to myself, having a happy time with man's best friend (my dog!), watching TV, or having a walk in the community with my parents.

地道表达

- regular schedule 常规日程
- recharge 恢复精力

(2) What did you do last weekend?

I had a wonderful day last Sunday with my sister who just came back from Japan. It had been ages since we last time saw each other, so we spent a whole day together. I treated her in her favourite restaurant and we enjoyed some exquisite dessert. In the afternoon, we went for a walk in the park, sharing our stories of the past few years. I showed her around the place I live, and I made us a fine supper. We had a nice day together.

亮点句型

- It has/had been ages since...

(3) What are you going to do next weekend?

I do not have a specific plan yet. Maybe I'll just stay at home and do some housework. I stay alone once or twice on weekends each month and I just enjoy the quietness and peacefulness. As to me, reading books, watching TV, or playing video games are all good ways to relax.

地道表达

- have a specific plan 有明确的计划

第三节 社交类 Social life

1. Birthdays

(1) How do children celebrate birthdays in your country?

For young children, they usually hold birthday parties under the guidance of their parents, so that the parents will know what activities to organise and whom they should invite. However, parents don't interfere with the detailed planning of the event, and children can enjoy themselves with all the creative games they come up with. For teenagers, they usually choose to eat out with friends, and then go to watch movies. Sometimes, they may also have home parties, like a dance party, film party or pillow fight.

地道表达

- under the guidance of...　在……的指导下
- interfere with　干涉
- come up with　想出
- pillow fight　枕头大战

(2) How did you celebrate your last birthday?

Unlike most people my age who go to bars with groups of friends, I spent my birthday with my parents, with quite a simple celebration, a cake, and some homemade food. I always value the precious time spent with my family. My last birthday was no exception to this rule. The slight difference was that I baked some cookies for my parents, to express my heartfelt gratitude for their constant support and care.

地道表达

- no exception　也不例外
- slight difference　细微差别
- heartfelt gratitude　衷心的感谢
- constant support　一贯的支持

(3) Is there a difference between the way you celebrated your birthday in the past and in the present?

There isn't much difference in particular. My birthday party is usually a small and personal family party, and the people I invite have been mostly the same across many years. We usually book a table at a relatively fancy restaurant since it is a once-a-year occasion.

However, I no longer feel as excited as before when receiving all the gifts during the party.

地道表达

- fancy restaurant　高级餐厅
- once-a-year occasion　一年一次的场合

2. Contact and communication

(1) How do you usually contact your friends?

I generally keep in touch with my friends by cellphone, saving time thanks to the direct communication. I can talk with them in depth, exchanging ideas immediately. Sometimes I use instant messaging through apps like WeChat or QQ, sending text messages or voice messages and even making video calls to each other.

地道表达

- keep in touch with...　与……保持联系
- instant messaging　即时通信

(2) In your country, do people contact each other in the same way compared to before?

Well, no, it is totally different. In the past, people could only write letters or send telegraphs, which were slow and inconvenient. But today, people can use many high-tech gadgets and electronic devices to contact people, mostly free of charge I should say.

地道表达

- high-tech gadget　高科技装置
- electronic device　电子器件

(3) Do you like to accept different opinions?

Yes, I do. I always respect other people's opinions. When they are right, I like to accept them into my life, which helps me make progress. I'm also willing to make a compromise or to come up with a new solution when a win-win situation is possible. I am not a stubborn person, so I'm quite open to others' suggestions and ideas.

地道表达

- make a compromise　做出让步
- be open to...　对……持开明态度
- win-win situation　双赢局面

3. Emails and letters

(1) Do you write many letters or emails?

As to handwritten letters, I do not write them often except on special occasions or for special people. I write formal letters to express appreciation, best wishes or apologies. However, emailing is quite my routine, and I write tens of emails every day to my teachers and classmates, confirming schedules and assigning tasks.

(2) Who do you usually write to?

My family members and friends are those who often hear from me. I like writing to them in person on special occasions, such as their birthdays, telling them how much I love them and how much I miss them if we are in different places. Luckily, they appreciate my letters, and promise to keep all of them carefully.

(3) How often do you write an email or a letter?

I have to write emails nearly every day, exchanging ideas with my classmates in the tutorial team, asking for help from my tutors, or submitting my assignment with finished documents attached. I only send handwritten letters once or twice each month, to express my best wishes to my friends on special occasions, because it is the best way to get my feelings across.

地道表达

- exchange ideas 交流想法
- submit assignment 提交作业
- get (...) across 被传达，被理解

(4) Is it hard to think of what to write?

It depends. For the letters to my family members and friends, I can never stop writing. However, for the formal letters to influential people like professors or would-be employers, especially those who determine whether I could be enrolled, promoted, or supported, I could spend many minutes deciding on a single word.

地道表达

- would-be employer 未来的老板
- enrol （使）加入，登记
- promote 晋升

(5) How do you feel when you receive a letter or email?

Well, I feel nothing in particular, if what I receive is work-related. I am most excited when I receive an offer from a dream school or a company I want to work for. Receiving handwritten letters or postcards from friends also brings joy to my life and makes my day. I can feel their affection and happiness in the words they have carefully written to me and I often read them many times.

地道表达

- nothing in particular 没什么特别的
- make my day 使我开心

(6) Which do you prefer, to make a phone call or write an email?

It depends. Making phone calls helps solve problems faster and urges people to make decisions immediately. However, writing an email gives the chance to rethink and edit the exact phrasing, so that the idea can get across clearly. It depends on whom I communicate with and what I want to talk about.

地道表达

- make decisions immediately 立即做出决定
- exact phrasing 精确措辞

(7) Do you think people will still write letters in the future?

Definitely. It is a rather personalised way of communication. People carefully write their thoughts down, taking a very long time to compose them. Compared to texts or emails, letters can best express their affections and emotions, especially to beloved family members and friends.

亮点句型

- Compared to texts or emails, letters could best express their affections and emotions...

地道表达

- personalised way of communication 个性化的交流方式
- beloved 深爱的

(8) How do you communicate with others at work—by email or is it more convenient to communicate face to face?

I tend to get the job done in a highly efficient way, so face-to-face conversation usually works better for immediate feedback and the exchange of different opinions. However, for proposals that my colleagues have to think over carefully or something that should be traceable, I have to use emails.

地道表达

- in a highly efficient way　以非常高效的方式
- immediate feedback　即时反馈
- proposal　建议，提议
- think over carefully　仔细考虑
- traceable　可追溯的

4. Friends

(1) When was the first time you met your best friend?

I met Tina, one of my best friends, at the age of three or four, though I can't remember exactly when. We became neighbours after our families had moved into the same community. We have known each other for two decades and she's always been my soulmate.

(2) What did you do together?

One of the common interests that bonded us closely was Lego blocks. As I remember, we spent most of our time playing those building blocks together and we could never get enough of them because there were so many possibilities they presented to our limitless imaginations. It was such fun for us to compete while playing.

地道表达

- bond　建立（与某人的）互信关系
- get enough of...　厌倦……

(3) Do you like to have a lot of friends or just several close friends?

I have high expectations for my friends, so having several close friends or even just one bosom buddy suits me better. I value quality friendship and I usually spend a lot of time with friends. I can share my thoughts with them, and they are lifelong company that I can share my life's ups and downs with.

地道表达

- bosom buddy　知心朋友
- ups and downs　起伏，起起落落

(4) Would you only make friends with people who are similar to you?

Most of my friends have the same or similar interests as me, which is the reason why we are good friends in the first place. However, I also make friends who have different personalities. These friends offer me different perspectives and opportunities to explore some new fields. This will help us enrich our understanding of each other, highlighting the importance of respecting individual differences.

地道表达
- in the first place 首先，一开始
- enrich 充实，使丰富
- respect individual differences 尊重个体差异

(5) Are your friends mostly your age or different ages?

Well, the majority of my friends are my age and we have the same interests and hobbies, which makes it easier for us to communicate and find common topics. But I also make friends with people of different ages because they could always share useful insights with me. The elders can give me valuable advice and the younger friends can bring me a lot of enjoyment.

地道表达
- common topics 共同话题
- share insights 分享见解

5. Gifts

(1) Do you like to receive gifts? Why?

Yes, I do. I'm always happy to get gifts from others, not only because of the gift itself, but also because of the best wishes that I feel from the gift. The confirmation that I am loved, cared for and valued is really heartwarming. Receiving gifts also helps me know how well the gift-givers know me, and it is a particularly happy moment if the gifts are exactly what I want. That is where the meaning of gifts lies.

亮点句型
- That is where the meaning of...lies.

地道表达
- gift-giver 赠送礼物的人

(2) What kind of gifts do you like to receive? Why?

I like the gifts that are handmade, instead of those selected in shops, because I cherish the meaning behind the gifts rather than their monetary value. Handmade gifts are a kind of personalised expression of affection. It's the time and emotion invested in them that make the gifts so special.

地道表达

- monetary value　金钱价值
- invested in...　投入（时间、精力等）

(3) Do you like giving gifts to people? Why?

Yes, I do. I need to express my love and care to my beloved friends by preparing gifts. Actually, giving makes me happier than getting, and I am happy to give my friends something helpful and meaningful, which provides me with a sense of accomplishment. I usually bake some cookies or make gadgets as gifts.

地道表达

- sense of accomplishment　成就感

6. Teamwork

(1) Do you like to work or study with others or just by yourself?

It depends on which studying assignment I have to complete. When working on some big challenging projects, I value the efficiency of teamwork, which allows us to finish the project much faster. However, when facing some personal academic problems, I will try to get them sorted by myself, for example, through browsing the web, looking things up in the dictionaries or reading some books.

地道表达

- get sth. sorted　解决某事

(2) What's the most important thing for teamwork?

I would say that communication among teammates is the most important. Team members can voice their opinions, share ideas, discuss, debate, persuade and compromise, respecting individual differences. Through communication, we can highlight others' opinions and settle disputes among team members, improving mutual understanding. Thus, no teamwork is perfect and complete without smooth communication.

亮点句型

- No...is perfect and complete without...

- highlight 突出，注意
- settle dispute 解决争端

7. Text messages

(1) Do you usually make phone calls or send texts?

I am kind of straightforward, so I usually make phone calls. It is quite direct and I can get things confirmed and finalised immediately, because people tend to directly give their opinions while talking over the phone. I value such efficiency.

地道表达

- kind of straightforward 比较率直
- get things confirmed and finalised 将事情确认并最终敲定

(2) Which do you prefer if there's something important, phone calls or text messages?

For something important, I prefer phone calls as I can get my ideas across more accurately through verbal and nonverbal clues, such as tones and emotions. These usually help me to communicate more efficiently.

地道表达

- the verbal and nonverbal clues 语言和非语言线索

(3) Do you think text messages can convey information well?

Text messages work well, because people can think twice and weigh their words carefully when editing their texts. A well-composed text usually contains more details than phone calls, though it is time-consuming.

地道表达

- work well 有效
- think twice 慎重考虑

第四节 技能类 Skills

1. Dancing

(1) Do you enjoy dancing?

Yes, I do enjoy dancing. It is the best way to release my emotion and passion, even if I am not a born dancer. It has strengthened my body and I have made a lot of friends with this common interest. I usually dance at my school's art centre, which helps me relieve pressure.

地道表达

- common interest 共同爱好
- relieve pressure 缓解压力

(2) How often do you dance?

I used to practise dancing every day, because I was once a good dancer in my childhood, and was trained as a professional for five years. However, I put a stop to all the practice and have focused on academic study for more than ten years. Now I am a bit clumsy and I think it is hard for me to restart.

地道表达

- train as a professional 受专业训练
- a bit clumsy 有点儿笨拙

2. Drawing

(1) What kind of pictures do you like to draw?

I like to draw still life images, like apples or bottles. When I go out sketching, I like to paint natural scenery. I also paint everyday things or people in the street, to reflect real life.

地道表达

- still life image 静物画

(2) Do you think drawing is difficult?

I believe nothing is difficult to a willing heart. I myself find it easy, as I study it diligently and I think it is full of fun. I have drawn day after day for years, and I'm quite good at drawing now.

- nothing is difficult to a willing heart　世上无难事，只怕有心人

(3) What is the difference between an adult and a child learning to draw?

The differences are huge and obvious. For some adults, they learn it systematically and with a sense of purpose. They will firstly confirm what they want to learn and which style they like, and then they start learning after full and deep communication with their teachers. For some young children, they just learn it under the guidance of their teachers.

地道表达

- huge and obvious　巨大且明显
- systematically　系统地
- with a sense of purpose　很有决心

3. Handwriting

(1) Which one do you prefer, writing by hand or using a computer?

I like both, I should say. Writing by hand gives me a lot of joy, because I can appreciate the beauty of Chinese handwriting and have an eye for the beauty of calligraphy. As to writing on the computer, I can write at will, with functions such as erasing, revising and rewriting based on rethinking. It is much more convenient.

地道表达

- have an eye for...　对……有鉴别力
- calligraphy　书法
- at will　随心所欲

(2) How often do you write by hand?

I have to take notes by hand every day and I make handwritten comments on book pages. I also spend a lot of time practising handwriting, dependent on the time available each day.

地道表达

- take notes　做笔记

(3) Can people judge a person from his or her handwriting?

In our culture, we do read a person by his or her handwriting. Usually it is a general practice to measure how well the writer is educated, whether or not the writer is resolute, patient, calm in personality, etc., though it is not absolutely precise. How some people write and what their handwriting is like could mirror a lot of things, which is a way to judge someone.

- resolute　果断的
- absolutely precise　绝对精确

(4) Do people write more or type more?

I should say they text more, using their mobile phones, instead of writing on paper. People also write on computers typing up files or replying to emails, which is much more convenient. However, people now seldom have the chance to write with a pen apart from signing their names.

地道表达

- apart from...　除了……

(5) Do you think handwriting will disappear?

No, I don't think so. In certain countries like China, calligraphy has been a form of art for thousands of years and has been appreciated by Chinese people since ancient times. Plus, people would never abandon handwriting, and it will be passed down to the future generations.

(6) How to improve handwriting?

One of the best ways is to use the copybooks and practise day after day, and people will soon get the hang of it. However, to reach a rather good level, people have to learn more, understand the culture and the meaning behind the characters, and know the differences between types and styles of calligraphy.

地道表达

- get the hang of...　掌握……的窍门

4. Painting

(1) Do you like painting or drawing?

I am kind of fond of painting, though I am not quite a good painter. I just like to paint, because when I am painting, I can fully focus. After finishing the work, I could also put the painting in one of my rooms as decoration.

(2) How often do you visit art galleries?

It depends. Every time I go to a new place, I always visit the local art galleries. Whenever there are exhibition series touring the country, I go to visit each of them when they come to my city, which means three or four in a row in just a couple of months.

地道表达

- art gallery 美术馆
- in a row 连续

(3) Is it easy to learn how to paint?

For those who are born painters, they are constantly inspired when painting and they can finish a masterpiece in hours, if they have gotten themselves systematically trained. For the beginners out of interest, they have to spend months practising line drawing before using paints and they will have to start by doing still life paintings.

地道表达

- out of interest 出于兴趣

5. Singing

(1) Do you often like to sing?

As to frequency, I should say 'seldom'. I am not good at singing, and I often sing out of tune. It is not an enjoyable experience for me to sing in front of other people. Even so, when I'm alone, I sometimes sing for fun.

地道表达

- the best bet 最好的选择

(2) When do you like to sing?

I usually sing in private. I always sing when I do the housework as though singing helps time go more quickly or maybe it's just to pretend that I really enjoy the work.

地道表达

- in private 私下里
- as though 就好像

(3) Is it difficult to sing well?

Well, naturally people will think it is as easy as pie for super stars like Michael Jackson to shake the world with their songs. However, it is actually their strong foundation of musical theoretical knowledge, their practice day after day, and their inherited talents that make their nice performance possible. For the ordinary people, though, some of us are sensitive to music and often practise singing, but we may never reach the level comparable to those who are naturally talented and systematically trained.

地道表达

- as easy as pie 易如反掌
- inherited talents 天生的才能

6. Swimming

(1) Do you like swimming?

Yes, I do like swimming. It allows me to keep fit and I also enjoy diving while swimming. Playing in the water is good fun. I should say I spend most of the summer in the pool. I can swim in different styles thanks to the systematic training I've received, and I have almost reached a professional swimming level.

地道表达

- systematic training 系统训练
- professional swimmer 职业游泳运动员

(2) Is it difficult to learn how to swim?

All things are difficult before they are learned. It is human nature to be kind of afraid of water at first, especially when young children start to learn swimming in a deep pool. What they have to do is remember what the coach has taught and demonstrated, and then challenge themselves and practise time after time. Once people get the hang of swimming, they can swim as fast as fish.

(3) Where do Chinese people like to go swimming?

In coastal areas, people enjoy swimming in seaside swimming districts where they can challenge the strong currents and rolling waves. In the inland cities, people go to stadiums or gyms where there are indoor or outdoor pools. People also tend to go to community pools more often, if there is one available, for the sake of convenience.

地道表达

- community pool 社区游泳池

第五节 交通类 Transport

1. Bicycles

(1) How often do you ride a bicycle?

At present, I do not ride a bike very often. I occasionally cycle with friends on sunny days for outdoor exercise. However, I used to ride my bicycle in my community compound to keep fit nearly every day, listening to my favourite music. It was kind of relaxing.

(2) Is it difficult to learn how to ride a bicycle?

It actually depends. For me, it was as easy as pie, no sweat I should say. I learned to cycle at a rather young age when I got a child-sized bike. It had one training wheel on each side, preventing me from losing my balance. I kept riding for months and after that, I could ride a real bicycle, the adult-sized one I mean.

地道表达
- no sweat　不费吹灰之力
- lose the balance　失去平衡

(3) When was the last time you used your bicycle?

It was last summer, when I attended a lakeside cycling event organised by my friends. In this fund-raising activity for environment protection, we wore uniforms and rode our bicycles with flags inserted behind the seats, with slogans calling for the protection of clean water and fresh air printed on them. We were trying to promote a more environmentally friendly lifestyle, which was meaningful and beneficial for everyone living in this region.

地道表达
- call for　呼吁
- environmentally friendly　环保的

(4) Would you ride bikes to work in the future?

It depends on how far it is from the place where I live to the place where I work. It also depends on the weather condition and air quality since it is not wise to cycle in haze and inhale polluted air outside.

2. Taxi

(1) Do you like taking a taxi?

No, I seldom take a taxi. I prefer the buses and subways. Taking a taxi costs too much money, and taxies may not travel fast in peak hours.

(2) In what kinds of situations do you take a taxi?

I take a taxi on many different occasions. Taking a taxi is the best option when I am pressed for time, so it means spending more money in exchange for time. When the weather is bad, I will take a taxi, so that I won't get wet, avoiding catching a cold.

地道表达
- in exchange for　交换
- get wet　被雨淋湿

(3) When was the first time you took a taxi?

It is hard to remember precisely my very first time taking a taxi. When I went to high school which was quite far from my home, I often took a taxi on rainy days. Also when I was in urgent situations or I was about to be late, I turned to cabbies for help.

地道表达
- turn to... for help　向……寻求帮助

3. Traffic

(1) What traffic problems are there in your city?

Well, there are many traffic problems that need solving in my city. The networks of the roads are not well planned, so in rush hour the traffic relies heavily on the help from traffic police. The traffic signals are never uniform here, which is potentially hazardous. Some of them change after a few seconds, while others change merely after one or two flashes, which increases the risk of accidents. There are few entrances to the overhead bridges, so both the roads on the ground and the roads on the bridges are over-crowded due to this inefficient design.

- well planned 被很好地规划
- rush hour 交通高峰期
- rely heavily on... 严重依赖……

- traffic signal 交通信号（灯）
- overhead bridge 高架桥

(2) How do traffic problems affect the citizens?

Firstly, traffic problems often influence people's schedule since they have to spend more time on route. Sometimes people have to work out alternative plans for detours for unexpected traffic jams, which is also more energy-consuming. Traffic problems also ruin people's mood, which would definitely influence their efficiency at work or in school for the whole day.

地道表达

- work out some plans for detours 制订出绕路的计划
- energy-consuming 消耗能量的

(3) How do traffic problems affect you?

Well, traffic problems such as traffic jams force me into the habit of thinking and planning in advance. Each time I go out, I have to think carefully and clearly, choosing the best route to take, calculating the time, and deciding which mode of transport is the best bet. And this habit really helps me save a lot of time.

地道表达

- force sb. into the habit of... 让某人形成……的习惯
- the best bet 最好的办法

4. Transportation

(1) What's the most popular means of transportation in your hometown?

I think the most popular means of transportation in my hometown would be the bus, because it can accommodate dozens of passengers at a time. It is environmentally friendly, cutting down carbon dioxide emissions. Besides, the network of buses extends to every corner of the city, so it is very convenient to go anywhere by bus.

地道表达

- cut down 减少
- carbon dioxide emission 二氧化碳排放

(2) Can you compare the advantages of planes and trains?

Planes have their own advantages that trains do not have and vice versa. Planes are much faster for long-distance travel, and people can enjoy the drinks and snacks provided on planes. Trains are more attractively priced, and people can also have a nice view of the natural scenery along the way.

地道表达
- long-distance travel　远途旅行
- be more attractively priced　价格更具吸引力

(3) Do you think people will drive more in the future?

I don't believe so. There will be less need to drive as people tend to live in areas close to where they work and study, and walking is more convenient than driving. People now tend to choose low-carbon ways to commute, such as riding shared bikes. More importantly, the development of the Internet offers the freedom to work and study from home, reducing the need for travelling to the workplace or school.

亮点句型
- There will be less need to...as people tend to...

(4) What will become the most popular means of transportation in your country?

Well, I should choose the subway. It combines all the advantages of public transportation and it particularly suits the situation of my country. It accommodates hundreds of passengers on each single departure, so it is the most productive in helping relieve traffic pressure. Thanks to the fixed timetable for departure and arrival, it saves time for commuters.

地道表达
- relieve traffic pressure　缓解交通压力
- departure and arrival　出发和到达

(5) Do you prefer public transportation or private transportation?

Presently speaking, the former is more my style. As a graduate fresh out of college, I do not have my own car yet, so I currently take public transportation more often. It helps me save money, and it is also convenient to go to each corner of the city with numerous routes available. Plus, whenever I have to take a taxi, I often require carpooling.

- fresh out of college　刚从大学毕业
- carpooling　拼车

(6) Should government encourage people to use public transportation?

Yes, and that is what the government should never stop doing. They should come up with incentives such as cheaper pricing for riding buses, subways and ferries. They should also work out some mandatory policies on the other side, such as increasing the taxes for gas and car ownership.

地道表达

- come up with...　想出，提出……
- mandatory policy　强制性政策

(7) How do most people travel to work where you live?

The city I live in is merely a medium-sized one, where the great majority of people work within the half-hour economic circle, in other words, in a ten-kilometre-radius around home. Therefore, a high proportion of people tend to ride their electric bikes or scooters. Still, some people choose to drive their private cars, which would often cost them more time compared to travelling by bike or taking commuter buses. So far, there is no subway system in my city, which is a little inconvenient. Personally speaking, I usually walk to work since my workplace is only one block away from home.

地道表达

- within the half-hour economic circle 在半小时经济圈内
- in a ten-kilometre-radius around home 在家周围十千米的范围内
- a high proportion of...　很大一部分……
- scooter　小型摩托车
- commuter bus　通勤公交车

第六节 描述类 Description

1. Animals

(1) Do you think we should protect animals?

Yes, definitely. We have to protect them because we respect life. The diversity of living creatures means a dynamic earth and better survival for humans. When we protect animals, we are better preserving the unspoiled nature in which the animals inhabit. Meanwhile, such measures ensure harmony between man and nature.

地道表达

- the diversity of living creatures 生物多样性
- the unspoiled nature 未被破坏的大自然
- the harmony between...and... ……和……之间的和谐

(2) Do you like pets?

Yes, they are nice family members, making me feel warm even though I have to spend a lot of time taking care of them. They are the best company to play or talk with, especially when I'm in a bad mood.

地道表达

- taking care of... 照顾好……
- in the bad mood 心情不好

(3) Do you like zoos?

It is hard to say. Zoos are prisons for some wild animals in a sense, depriving them of their freedom. It is a pity that those animals will have to spend their lives in cages. On the other side, however, zoos provide shelter for some endangered species to survive and breed.

亮点句型

- It is a pity that...

地道表达

- in a sense 在一定程度上说
- provide shelter for... 为……提供庇护所
- endangered species 濒危物种

(4) How do you feel about visiting a zoo?

I'm happy every time I go to the zoo, as the zoo I frequent has pretty good facilities. It offers the animals good living conditions to enjoy their life. As tourists, we can also find places in the zoo to grab a cup of coffee and have a good rest. However, I always feel pity for the caged animals.

地道表达

- grab a cup of coffee   喝杯咖啡
- have a good rest   好好休息

2. Apps

(1) Describe an app in your computer or phone.

I would like to share Didi-Bike with you. It is one of the most popular applications thanks to the convenience it offers. You can use it to locate the nearest bike, scan the QR code, unlock the bike, cycle to your destination and then just park it in a nearby designated area. This is the epitome of convenient, healthy and low-carbon transportation.

地道表达

- scan the QR code   扫描二维码
- designated area   指定区域
- convenient, healthy and low-carbon transportation   便捷、健康和低碳的交通

(2) Is it convenient to use apps?

Yes, it is. I use apps to order takeaway food, which saves time and energy compared to eating out. I can also use other apps to buy books without having to go to the bookstore. What I need to do is just type in my needs in the search box and all the books that fit my criteria are listed on the screen with comments and ratings. Besides, I use e-map apps to best plan my routes when going out, avoiding traffic jams.

地道表达

- eat out   出去吃饭
- type in   键入
- comments and ratings   评价与打分

(3) What are the drawbacks to using apps?

Well, of course there are some negative aspects. Since apps are very capable, people tend to overly rely on them, and believe what the apps recommend without independent thinking. There are also a lot of game apps, which may attract people to spend too much time playing rather than working or studying.

(4) Is using an app more acceptable for young people than the elderly?

Yes, it is. Young people are more prone to try new things and they are quick learners. On the contrary, the elderly are usually unwilling to use new things since they have gotten used to how they live and work for decades. It is quite hard for old dogs to learn new tricks.

地道表达

- be more prone to... 更倾向于……
- get used to... 习惯于……
- on the contrary 相反

3. Computers

(1) What kinds of computers are popular in China?

Laptops, of course. They are light, portable and convenient, suitable for those who need to take their computers to different places to study and work. High-end computers are also popular since they are favoured by people who are really fond of computer games.

地道表达

- high-end 高级的，高端的
- be fond of... 喜欢……

(2) What do you usually use your computer for?

As a student, I mainly use my computer for study, such as building models to analyse data collected, writing essays or taking on-line courses. I also use my computer for relaxation. I play games, watch videos or talk online with friends through my computer.

4. Flowers

(1) Which/What is your favourite flower?

I like lotus flowers the most, because their pinkish paddles are pure and clean, coming out of mud unsoiled. The lotus flowers bring peace to my mind while I spend minutes gazing at them and appreciating them. Lotus seeds are not only nutritious food ingredients, but also good raw materials for traditional Chinese medicine. The stems and leaves can be used as medicine as well.

- food ingredient 食材
- raw material 原材料
- traditional Chinese medicine 中药

(2) Do you think flowers are important?

I think flowers play an important role in our lives. People use flowers as the medium to express different feelings on different occasions. Flowers are always nice gifts as a general practice. It is quite suitable to choose a bunch of flowers, especially when we are not sure the likes and the dislikes of the other person, to show our respect and politeness.

地道表达

- play an important role 起重要作用
- general practice 常见做法
- a bunch of... 一束……

5. History

(1) Which historical period do you think is the most important in your country?

Well, all periods matter, because I think every period contributes to what the country is today. However, I believe that the Qin Dynasty is the most important period, because it is the first unified feudal dynasty in Chinese history. During this period, the currency, characters and weights and measures were unified, which facilitated the exchange of ideas and goods between different parts of the country.

地道表达

- contribute to... 促成……
- feudal dynasty 封建王朝
- weights and measures 度量衡
- facilitate 促进，促使

(2) Do you think history matters in a country's future development?

Yes, it does. History acts as a mirror, reflecting how the nation has developed and how the people's thoughts have evolved. History tends to repeat itself, so we can predict the future using what has happened as good guidance and reference. Thus, we can be better prepared for the future.

地道表达

- act as... 起到……的作用
- predict the future 预测未来
- guidance and reference 指导与参考

6. Science

(1) Do you like science?

Yes, I do. Science promotes human development. It also offers answers to mysterious questions. I am interested in science-related questions and I can get a lot of joy exploring them.

(2) Were there many science classes when you were young?

In primary school, we had some general science courses. They were just for beginners, primarily arousing our curiosity and making us think about the theories behind scientific discoveries. In middle school, there were science courses like Physics and Chemistry, through which we could learn how various things react to each other.

地道表达
- arouse one's curiosity 引起某人的好奇
- react with each other 互相反应

(3) Did you like science classes when you were young?

Yes, I did, because science classes were full of fun. I didn't have to memorise texts mechanically and could solve problems through the science of deduction and analysis. Once I got the hang of it, I could not get enough of it.

地道表达
- science of deduction 科学推理

7. Sunny days

(1) Do you like sunny days?

Yes, definitely. Sunny days make people feel cheerful, and good weather allows people to do more outdoor activities, such as camping, hiking, mountain-climbing, surfing, etc.

(2) Do you like to stay at home or go outside when the weather is great?

I think it is such a waste to stay at home in good weather. In my city, most of the days are kind of hazy and foggy. I always manage to make the best use of good days cycling, having a picnic, or walking my dog. And if it is a bit hot during summer days, I could go swimming.

- make the best use of... 充分利用······

(3) Are there many sunny days in your hometown?

In my hometown, there are a lot of sunny days in spring, autumn and winter. During summer, it rains a lot.

8. Teachers

(1) What kinds of teachers do you like the most?

I prefer the easy-going types. I like the feeling of being treated like a friend, which makes me more willing to learn. Those teachers are approachable and easy to talk with, and I also want to keep in contact with them after graduation.

地道表达

- easy-going 随和的
- approachable 和蔼可亲的

(2) Who was your favourite teacher when you were young?

I should say my English teacher, and she has always been my favourite teacher. I enjoyed her teaching style, which was interesting and informative. Her patience deeply touched me, and whenever we made some mistakes in English usage, she would always offer us some help without reprimanding us.

地道表达

- interesting and informative 有趣且信息丰富
- reprimand 斥责

(3) Which teacher helped you the most?

My English teacher helped me the most. She is a knowledgeable and experienced instructor who offered us guidance and led us in playing games concerning English learning. She made endless efforts to encourage us to interact with each other and exchange ideas.

地道表达

- knowledgeable and experienced 知识渊博，经验丰富
- make endless efforts 不遗余力

(4) Would you like to be a teacher in the future?

No, I wouldn't. Teaching is quite demanding. To be a teacher, one has to be patient, enthusiastic, knowledgeable and responsible. It is not my style, and I would rather work in a business organisation, where there would be more chances to gain higher income and more training opportunities.

地道表达

- demanding 要求高的
- patient 有耐心的
- enthusiastic 热情的
- responsible 有责任心的
- higher income 较高的收入
- training opportunity 培训机会

Notes

第七节　娱乐类 Entertainment

1. Films

(1) Do you like watching films?

Yes, I do. As a cinema goer, I should say I am a film addict. By watching films I can relax while enjoying wonderful stories and music.

地道表达

- cinema goer　常去电影院的人
- film addict　电影迷

(2) Do you like foreign films?

Yes, I like foreign films very much, especially those well-made Hollywood films with excellent plots, sound effects and 3D techniques. I can never get enough of the serials like *Iron Man*, *Spider-Man*, etc.

地道表达

- sound effect　音效
- get enough of...　厌烦……
- *Iron Man*　《钢铁侠》
- *Spider-Man*　《蜘蛛侠》

(3) How often do you go to a cinema to watch a film?

It is primarily determined by whether the film I'm interested in is on, so I go to cinemas more frequently during summer vacations, during which there are a series of good films released. When the film seasons are over, I just go there on a monthly basis.

地道表达

- release　发行（电影、书等）
- on a monthly basis　每月

(4) What was the first film that you watched?

Honestly, I cannot remember the very first film that I watched since I was too young at the time, and it would be difficult to precisely recall when, where and what. However, the first one that impressed me was *Forrest Gump*, which is full of positive power. The film shocked me and the spirit of Forrest Gump inspired me a lot.

地道表达

- *Forrest Gump* 《阿甘正传》

2. Music

(1) When do you listen to music?

I listen to music almost all day long. I wear my headphones whenever I can, so I listen to music while walking, cycling, exercising and riding. I also play some light music as background music while reading books or taking a nap.

地道表达

- wear headphones 戴耳机
- light music 轻音乐

(2) What kinds of music do you like to listen to?

I like to listen to pop music for relaxing, and I usually listen to light music before going to bed. But I prefer heavy metal music when I am stressed out.

地道表达

- pop music 流行音乐
- stressed out 极度焦虑的
- heavy metal music 重金属音乐

(3) Have you ever been to a musical performance?

I have been to a symphony concert in Beijing, which was pretty much a joyful experience in my life. The concert was a supreme banquet of art and music. To a music lover and an instrument player like me, I admire the performers' musical talents. The pieces they performed were primarily the works of Bach, my favourite musician and composer. It was an impressive performance.

地道表达

- symphony concert 交响音乐会
- a supreme banquet 盛宴
- a joyful experience 一件乐事
- musical talent 音乐才华

3. Newspapers

(1) Do you often read newspapers?

Yes, I read them quite often. My parents and I have a habit of reading newspapers in the morning, during breakfast time to be precise, for some up-to-date info.

地道表达

- to be precise 确切地说
- up-to-date info 最新信息

(2) Why do (you think) people read newspapers?

For many people, reading newspapers has been a general habit for years. They read newspapers for information, to learn new techniques or even to catch up on gossip for fun. Some people focus mainly on the sports section.

(3) Which do you prefer reading, magazines or newspapers?

I prefer to read magazines, because the contents of magazines are more diversified and entertaining. Besides, the print quality of magazines is better. I enjoy some popular science magazines like *National Geographic*, and I'm attracted to its amazingly beautiful photographs.

地道表达

- diversified 多元化的
- entertaining 令人愉快的

(4) How old were you when you first started to read newspapers?

My father often read newspapers to me when I was five, with explanations through some simple words. When I was a third grader, I had to read some newspapers as an assignment. Gradually, such mandatory tasks became my daily routine, and I finally fell in love with reading newspapers.

地道表达

- third grader 三年级学生
- assignment 作业；任务
- mandatory task 强制性任务
- daily routine 日常事务

4. TV programmes

(1) Do you watch TV quite often?

Yes, every day. It is my regular schedule to watch TV from 7 pm to 9 pm with my parents, indulging myself in some live news, talk shows or soap operas.

(2) How long will you allow your kids to watch TV?

I think that children should be encouraged to watch news for half an hour every day, and be allowed to watch their favourite TV programmes for another half hour. I won't allow my kids to watch TV for too long. They should put most of their energy into study or sports.

Notes

第八节 喜好类 Likes

1. Art

(1) Do you like art?

Yes, I like art, and I like to appreciate art works, such as paintings, sculptures or buildings, etc. I myself practise drawing sometimes, and I think artistic pursuits such as drawing and painting can help cultivate my tastes and make me think creatively.

地道表达

- appreciate art works 欣赏艺术作品
- artistic pursuit 艺术追求
- sculpture 雕塑

(2) Do you think art classes are necessary?

Yes, I think art classes are quite necessary, and students should be required to take art lessons. Through taking art classes, students can learn how to appreciate art work. Moreover, students can learn more about different cultures represented by different art work.

(3) What can you learn from western paintings?

From western paintings, I can learn a lot about western culture, history, and religious stories. I can also learn about different western painting schools popular in different ages, such as baroque art, neoclassicism and impressionism, etc.

地道表达

- western painting schools 西方绘画流派
- neoclassicism 新古典主义
- baroque art 巴洛克艺术
- impressionism 印象主义

(4) What benefits can you get from painting as a hobby?

Firstly, painting helps me build patience and self-control since it usually takes a long time to finish a painting. Secondly, I can acquire knowledge on art history, art schools and painting techniques, and learn anecdotes about painting masters. Thirdly, I can express emotions through painting, and I always enjoy myself when I paint.

地道表达

- build patience and self-control 培养耐
  心和自制力
- painting technique 绘画技巧
- anecdote 轶事
- painting master 绘画大师

2. Books

(1) Do you like reading books?

Yes. I like reading books, because it can broaden my outlook and enrich my mind. I want to be an interesting person through constant book reading.

(2) Did you read much when you were a child?

Yes, if I may say so. I was crazy about fairy tales in my childhood. I just liked the mysterious plots, the positive miracles as well as the adventures the characters experienced. Reading those books was a must before bedtime, taking me into a wonderland in my dreams. Now, there are still piles of fairy tale books on my bookshelf.

地道表达

- be crazy about... 痴迷于……
- fairy tale 神话故事
- mysterious plot 神秘的情节
- a must 必须做（或看、买等）的事

(3) Do young children like reading books?

I don't think so. Children now tend to watch popular films, cartoons or TV programmes rather than reading a good book from cover to cover. They are profoundly influenced by the fast-food culture and it is hard for them to sit and get down to reading.

地道表达

- read...from cover to cover 把……从头
  读到尾
- fast-food culture 快餐文化
- get down to... 开始干……，着手做……

(4) Do you like reading novels or not?

I used to read a lot of novels for fun when I was a middle school student. The novels I read provided elaborate plots and various characters, offering fascinating insights into real life. However, I am now much busier, so I've shifted my preference towards novellas, each of which is less than a hundred pages. I can still gain a lot of insights, though they are not as enjoyable as novels.

地道表达

- elaborate plot 精心设计的情节
- novella 中篇小说

(5) Paper novel or web novel, which do you prefer?

I prefer paper novels. It feels quite good to hold a real book in my hands and I can immerse myself in the story. I can take the book to any place, and read it when I am in the subway or when I am lining up to wait for my turn. Though web novels are much more convenient and potentially cheaper, they do not fit my reading style: they usually update daily, and when I finish one episode, my keenness for the next one tortures me a lot.

地道表达

- immerse oneself in... 沉浸于……
- episode （小说）片段
- line up 排队
- keenness 渴望，热切心情

3. Colours

(1) What is your favourite colour?

Blue has always been my favourite colour, as it reminds me of the sky and the ocean, and the colour blue can always make me feel calm and sober. A lot of my own belongings are blue-coloured, such as my bicycle, my pen and most of my clothes.

地道表达

- remind sb. of sth. 提醒某人某事
- belongings 财物
- sober 清醒的

(2) What can you learn about a person from the colours they like?

Well, in my opinion, people's preference of colours has something to do with their personalities and the moods they are in. For example, people who prefer dark colours, such as black, tend to be prudent and less pretentious, while people who like bright colours, such as yellow, seem to be more energetic and optimistic.

地道表达

- prudent 谨慎的
- pretentious 自负的

(3) Do any colours have a special meaning in your culture?

Well, some colours have different meanings in our culture, which have been pretty fixed for thousands of years. For example, red represents luck and happiness, and is used in all the ceremonial celebrations like weddings and festivals. White is often associated with death and funerals. Golden yellow has been regarded as the colour of royalty, and purple symbolises nobility.

(4) When you are buying something, is the colour important to you?

Colour is one of the factors that will affect my decision when I am buying things, but I would usually take many things into consideration, like the design, the price, the after-sales service and so on. When it is quite a good buy, colour is not that important.

地道表达
- take...into consideration 将……考虑在 内
- after-sales service 售后服务
- a good buy 合算的买卖

(5) Do you usually wear clothes in your favourite colour?

It usually depends on what I have to do, where I have to go and whom I have to meet. It is fine to wear my favourite red going to parties, or during festivals. However, I will definitely wear some dark colours like black on official occasions, or some light colours while doing sports.

(6) Is colour very important to you when you are buying clothes?

I tend to choose clothes with colours that suit the colour of my skin, my age and my personality. I will firstly consider some light shades because they make me look neat and fresh.

4. Subjects

(1) What subjects do you like?

I am a math person and I particularly like numerical analysis. I am also fond of physics, which studies the laws of general motion and basic structure of matter.

(2) How do you enjoy the courses in your major?

I am majoring in Advanced Math and the courses related are really hard to learn and tiring. I have to devote all my free time to preparing and reviewing the lessons, doing homework and discussing problems with my classmates. However, I still enjoy taking these courses because it is challenging and gives me a sense of achievement.

地道表达

- devote...to...   把……用于……

(3) What subjects are you studying?

So far, I have been working on ten subjects this semester, including Chinese, English, Politics, Math, Physics, Chemistry, Geography, History, Fine Art and Music.

(4) What is the first subject learned by children in your country?

Of course, it is Chinese. Children begin to learn this subject formally or informally from a very young age, even prior to kindergarten. They begin to learn words from their parents, and some of them can even write some words before primary education.

地道表达

- formally or informally   正式或非正式地
- prior to...   在……之前

(5) What was your favourite subject in secondary school?

Math was my favourite subject since I am kind of talented at mathematics. I always enjoyed solving questions with multiple solutions instead of memorising the standard methods from textbooks, and this made me more confident. I also value its role as a prerequisite for other science courses, which pushes me further in my mathematical learning.

地道表达

- be kind of talented at...   在……方面有几分天分
- prerequisite   必备条件
- multiple solutions   多种解法

Notes

Part 2 冲刺技巧

IELTS

SPEAKING

一、Part 2 简介

雅思口语考试的 Part 2 对基础薄弱的考生来说是一个很大的挑战。Part 2 要求准备时间为 1 分钟，回答时长为 1～2 分钟。题目的设计分为四大主题，主要包括人物类、物品类、事件类和地点类。在每个大类下又可以细化为各种小类，如人物类可以具体分为高龄、同龄、低龄等不同的类别，也可以按照熟悉与陌生、知名与普通等进行分类。在雅思考试中，无论是口语话题、写作话题还是听力及阅读机经题库，题目的数量都是有限的。参加雅思考试的人次逐年增加，雅思考试一年会举行 40 次左右，每个月大约 2～4 场考试，试题存在着大量的迭代性重复。

二、Part 2 考查重点

对于考生来说，在考场上进行学术化的话题论述确实是有难度的。Part 2 的话题在能力考核方面要求考生具有描述特点及细节的能力、叙述经过的能力、评价相关现象及行为的能力、比较与评判的能力等。在语法、句型、词汇等方面，Part 2 也会对考生进行全方位的能力测评。在这些综合能力测评之后，口语考试还会考评考生在考场上的发挥与表达，使用语言表述思想时的语言效率、信息有效性及交互能力。在考场上无论语速如何，考生答题时一定要有逻辑、有层次，同时要让考官觉得你确实是在边讲边组织语言，尽量做到思维敏捷，语言自然、流畅。

三、Part 2 题卡

Part 2 的考题是以题卡（Cue Card）的形式出现的。在考场上考官持有多个本场考试使用的题卡，并在这些题卡中随机抽取考生在 Part 2 要讲的题目。题目由一个主话题提纲配合四个延展提纲构成。为了防止考生准备各种套路模板，考官在出题方面可谓煞费苦心。目前 Part 2 题目的主话题提纲基本上包含三个关键点。例如下面这个题卡中的主话题提纲是"描述你在高中数学课上学到的一项有用的技能"，这里不仅是要求描述"技能"，还附加了两个限定："高中数学课上学到的"和"有用的"。

Describe a useful skill you learned in a math class from your high school.

You should say:

    what the skill was

    how you learned it

    who taught you

and explain why it was useful to you.

除了主话题提纲，后面还跟着四个细化延展提纲，构成回答的方向。这样一方面可以帮助考生确定答题的方向，另一方面这种明确的提纲可以更有效地测评考生在相同题目框架内表现出的语言水平和思路、观点的差异。基础较弱的考生基本上会倾向于把每个提纲当作一个问题进行基本的回答，这样简单的回应内容会比较单薄，很可能不到一分钟就讲完了。基础稍好的考生可以对题目提纲进行有效的回应，对相关的小提纲细化延展、展开论述。对于语料库丰富、思路开阔且才思敏捷的考生来说，每一个提纲都可以进行有效的充分延展，答题时能够将各个层面的内容有机融合，而非只是一两个单句的回答。回应一个题目提纲的几个句子形成的一个语意组合，笔者称之为"语组"，题目中的四个提纲应该通过不同的"语组"与之回应。在组织回应四个提纲时，要充分延展的是最后一个提纲。这个小提纲通常要求考生对意义、影响、喜欢的原因等进行深度探讨，是整个答案中的重点内容。

四、Part 2 思路延展打样

下面我们来通过一道 Part 2 的题目来看答题时应如何回应，提纲如何延展，是使用统一风格还是变换风格，具体要用哪些句型，内容如何衔接等。

Describe an interesting historic place.

You should say:

    what it is

    where it is located

    what you can see there now

and explain why this place is interesting.

答案的第一句一定要扣题，给出明确的回应性答案：

● The interesting historic place I would like to talk about in more details at this moment is...

- I would like to single out the..., because it means a lot to me/the city/our nation.
- I'd like to say something about a historic place named...

第一个延展提纲是 what it is。这个提纲字面上看有些过于简单，而且和前面的主话题提纲是重复的。如果想要进行有效的拓展，可以学会把单一的内容加层面、浅显的内容加深意。在这道题目中，对于 what it is 这个提纲，既可以讲其现在的功能、性质、用途及建筑风格，也可以讲其以前是做什么用的。这一方法笔者称之为"有效的分层"。

- It is now, as you can see, just a park for people to relax with springs and some ancient architecture built in the Qing Dynasty.
- It is just a park for local residents and tourists to visit and have fun...
- However, few people know that in ancient times, about...years ago to be exact, it was..., used as...

接下来，讲下一个提纲时可以考虑使用不同的表述方式。例如：

- Next, the location.
- Well, let's move on to its location.
- Can you imagine that/Few people know that its location was once of great strategic significance.
- It is located in the city centre, which is surrounded by plenty of high rises.
- It is not far away from my home, and I can walk there in twenty minutes.

考生如果能熟练应用一些较为学术的句型，例如对雅思听力原文中的句子进行模仿和应用，可以为自己的回答增色。例如针对第三个延展提纲：

- The first and the most impressive thing people will see when they go there is that..., which...
- However, I believe the...is the thing more worth watching, because...

最后一个提纲就需要论述对于不同的人来说这样的历史建筑有何种意义和特点，针对这一提纲的回答可以分层次详细论述。例如：

- For those who come just for fun, what they see is just the beauty of the scenery. However, for people who are interested in history, there are many things worth appreciating and exploring, such as...
- There are primarily three aspects that make this place interesting...

五、Part 2 考场流程

在雅思口语 Part 2 考试的考场上，考官会向考生解释答题的要求、准备的时长、记号笔和白板的使用说明，并告知考生答题中考官有可能打断或中止考生的答题。考官解释完答题的要求后，会给考生 Part 2 题目的题卡。一分钟计时结束后，考生开始答题，考官在聆听 1 ～ 2 分钟之后会打断或中止考生的答题。在考生开始答题时，考官会在聆听的同时给出一些回应，也许是肯定和鼓励的眼神和表情，也许是皱眉或者耸肩。不管考官给出何种反应，考生都不必太过在意，专注于自己的回答即可。答题经验少、易紧张的考生可以使用考场上所提供的记号笔和白板，记下一些关键的点或提示词，可以有效避免在考场上由于过度紧张而忘记后面的内容。

Notes

Part 2 机经话题分类实战

IELTS

SPEAKING

第一节 物品类 Objects

1. An interesting magazine

Describe an interesting magazine.

You should say:

what the magazine specialises in

what information it contains

who will read this magazine

and explain why you think this magazine is interesting.

思路延展

第一语组：明确"杂志名称"，描述其品类、发行周期等；

第二语组：回应"杂志的专业方向及内容"，多维度分层延展具体内容和评价；

第三语组：具体回应"读者的分类"，延展"对不同读者的意义与帮助"等；

第四语组：回应"杂志有意思的具体原因"。

高分范例

I'd like to talk about a monthly magazine named *World Architecture*. This periodical can be a yearly subscription or bought at magazine booths all over China. Of all the magazines that I have read, this magazine fascinates me the most with its rich contents. It is a specialised and academic periodical that has always been its field leader. It outlines the most up-to-date research and study on architecture, illustrated by precise yet lively words and colourful pictures. I was so engrossed in this magazine that I could not put it down until I completed it. The section that introduces great architects has always been my favourite, as I can feel the personal strength in the field of architecture, which inspires me to work harder and reach their level in the future. This magazine is not only popular among students who major in architectural design like me, but is also enjoyed by some enthusiasts who are obsessed with visiting architecture with mind-blowing design features, constantly searching for their next destination thanks to the magazine. I often reread the previous issues and get something new out of them, appreciating the architecture anew with a brand new perspective. I always call this magazine my personal teacher of architecture and I believe it will continue guiding me across my career as an architect.

亮点句型

- I'd like to talk about a monthly magazine named...
- Of all the magazines that I have read, this magazine fascinates me the most with...
- The section that introduces great architects is always my favourite, as I can feel the personal strength in the field of architecture, which inspires me to work harder and reach their level in the future.

地道表达

- monthly 按月发行的
- subscription 订阅
- up-to-date 最新的
- be engrossed in... 全神贯注于……

- put it down 放下，停止
- mind-blowing design 令人惊叹的设计
- reread 重读

2. Clothes

Describe clothes the other people have given you.

You should say:

what kind of clothing it is

what it is like

who gave it to you

and explain why it is important to you.

思路延展

第一语组：明确具体的"衣服"，与 what kind 结合；

第二语组：结合"类型与样式"进行回应，对下文内容进行铺垫；

第三语组：具体回应"赠送人"，以及衣服蕴含的意义；

第四语组：重点回应"对自己比较有重要意义的方面"，如家人的关爱、想法的满足等。

高分范例

I have gotten countless clothes from my parents, my grandparents and other relatives throughout my childhood and adolescence. However, the piece of clothing I received from my parents on my 18th birthday meant a lot to me. It was a traditional Chinese costume in the style of the Han Dynasty. Unlike the T-shirts and skirts we usually wear today, this costume looked like a purple robe with extremely wide cuffs, decorated with intricate embroidery depicting a white crane soaring across the sky. My parents had this costume tailored with patterns, colours and accessories all to my liking, and gave it to me on that special occasion as a surprise. I shrieked with excitement when I first laid my eyes on the costume since it was my dream outfit. It is a pity that I only get to wear it in private, and there are very few occasions during which I can show off this costume. However, more and more people have joined in the effort to advocate traditional Chinese culture, so maybe I will have the chance to wear it on a daily basis in the future. The costume is not only a garment, but also the embodiment of Chinese culture.

亮点句型

- Unlike..., this costume looks like..., decorated with...
- It is a pity that..., and there are very few occasions during which I can show off this costume.
- The costume is not only..., but also...

地道表达

- countless 无数的
- adolescence 青少年时期
- mean a lot to sb. 对某人来说意义非凡
- in private 私下里
- show off 炫耀
- advocate 提倡
- embodiment 体现

3. In-home equipment

Describe a piece of equipment in your home.

You should say:

what it is

how often you use it

who you usually use it with

and explain why it is important to you.

思路延展

第一语组：首先明确具体的"设备"，与提纲中的 what it is 结合；

第二语组：回应"使用的频次"，结合使用的原因与用途展开；

第三语组：具体回应"使用的人"，讲述对使用者的帮助；

第四语组：重点回应"重要意义"，如省时、省力、高效等。

I'd like to talk about the smart sweeping robot in my home. It is pretty flat and round, about 35 centimetres in diameter, and it does not take up much space but can complete all the floor cleaning work all by itself. I use it nearly every day. All I need to do is simply click an icon in my mobile phone app, and then the robot will take the order to sweep the floor. Before I bought this robot, my parents frequently had fights over the division of household chores at home and complained about having no free time to relax. But now, with the help of the robot, they can devote more time to relaxation. The robot is important to me since it has been our most frequently used home appliance. First, it is quite intelligent. It will automatically scan the room first, and then calculate the routes so that it can sweep the floor in the shortest time possible. When it is low on power, it will automatically go back to the charger and then continue to work from the place where it had stopped after having recharged. Secondly, it helps save my time, lightening my housework burden, so that I can better concentrate on more important things and have more time to relax.

亮点句型

- All I need to do is...
- ...so that it can sweep the floor in the shortest time possible.

地道表达

- 35 centimetres in diameter 直径为 35 厘米
- take up 占用
- division of household chores 家务劳动分工
- low on power 低电量

4. Something that made you happy

Describe something you bought that made you feel happy.

You should say:

what it is

when you bought it

why you bought it

and explain how you felt when buying it and what you felt happy about.

思路延展

第一语组：首先明确"所买的物品"，与提纲中的 what it is 结合；

第二语组：回应"购买的时间"等细节，还原购买的场景信息；

第三语组：具体回应"购买的原因"，描述物品的功能和优点；

第四语组：重点回应"购买时和购买后的感受"。

高分范例

Honestly speaking, I am kind of cautious when shopping. I tend to think twice, especially when I want something decent but expensive. As to the happiest purchase I've ever made, I would like to single out a pan I bought, though it cost an arm and a leg. I went to Silver Plaza one day, with the specific purpose of getting myself a really good pan, preferably a name brand with an attractive price. My budget was 500 RMB, but I didn't mind raising it to 1000 RMB for something really good. I went straight to the counter selling Demeyere cookware. A shopping assistant nearby was showing customers the advanced manufacturing techniques used to create first-class cookware with persuasive sales talk, and I dropped by for a few minutes. The shopping assistant even offered me a chance to try the pan myself right on the spot. Though I was not good at cooking, I made delicious food with just a few minutes' work, all thanks to the excellent pan. This quickly convinced me that in order to cook fantastic food, I need to use not only the best ingredients but also the best pan possible, and thus, I just bought the pan without a second thought. I have been enjoying the powerful capacities of the pan. Although the price was a little beyond my budget, it was well worth it. What's more, they offered a culinary course for me to attend, through which I could make some good friends while learning. In short, it was a very pleasant shopping experience.

亮点句型

- As to the happiest purchase I've ever made, I would like to...
- What's more, they offered a culinary course for me to attend, through which I could make some good friends while learning.

地道表达

- honestly speaking 说实话
- think twice 再三思考
- something decent 像样的东西
- cost an arm and a leg 价格昂贵
- with the specific purpose 有着明确的目的
- raise 提高
- drop by 停留
- on the spot 当场
- thanks to... 归功于……
- culinary course 烹饪课程

5. Something you bought

Describe something you bought but do not use often.

You should say:

　　what it is

　　when and where you got it

　　what made you buy it

and explain why you rarely use it.

思路延展

第一语组：首先明确具体的"物品"，与提纲中的 what it is 结合；

第二语组：回应"购买的时间与地点"，描述消费的场景；

第三语组：具体回应"购买的理由"，可以讲述做决定前的思想过程；

第四语组：重点回应"不经常使用的原因"，如个人惰性、产品有问题、体验不佳等。

高分范例

This question is kind of hard for me, because I am kind of cautious and I always think twice before buying things, asking myself whether I will make good use of what I am going to buy over and over again. So the only thing I can come up with at this moment, which I seldom use or gave up using a long time ago, is a machine I bought for losing weight. I bought it after I caught a commercial for it by chance at home. The sales person claimed that it could help burn calories through vibration. I dismissed it as a fraud, but when some celebrities were invited to the television programme, telling their successful stories of losing weight, my conviction wavered a little. The programme then claimed that people on average lost five kilograms each month by using the machine for just an hour per day, and with the discount offered during the limited time, the machine only cost around 100 RMB. This really pushed me to order the machine right away since there was no harm in trying it, right? However, when I received the goods, just like my initial thought, the machine was packed in a plain cardboard box without even an instruction booklet. The effect was not as significant as I was assured. Thankfully, the machine did not cost a fortune and the whole experience was a lesson learned. The machine has been left in the basement without being used again, and I won't fall for the same kind of fraud ever again.

亮点句型

● So the only thing I can come up with at this moment, which I seldom use or gave up using a long time ago, is a machine I bought for losing weight.

- However, when I received the goods, just like my initial thought, the machine was packed in a plain cardboard box without even an instruction booklet.

地道表达

- make good use of... 充分利用……
- by chance 随机
- dismiss it as a fraud 认为这是欺诈
- the discount offered 提供的折扣
- instruction booklet 说明书
- cost a fortune 价格很高

6. Something you shared

Describe something you shared with other people.

You should say:

what it is

who you shared it with

why you shared it with others

and explain how you felt about sharing.

思路延展

第一语组：首先明确具体的"物品"，与提纲中的 what it is 结合；

第二语组：回应"一起分享的人"，说明人物的身份、关系和其他信息；

第三语组：具体回应"分享的原因"，如提供帮助、使生活更加便利等；

第四语组：重点回应"自己的感受"，乐于分享，能够帮助他人，增进人们之间的情感等。

高分范例

I would like to talk about my room offer to one of my classmates, Lily. It was last summer when she came to our city after graduation from middle school. Her reservation for a room at a nearby hotel was cancelled due to mishandling on the hotel side. Though she got a refund for all the booking fees, she couldn't find a hotel with vacant rooms nearby because it was the high season in our city. Most of the hotels were fully occupied and some hostels doubled the prices of their rooms. So when she turned to me for help, I invited her to stay over at my house for one night. We shared my bedroom and I offered my bed to her, so I just slept on the daybed. People always say 'sharing means caring' and my simple act of sharing my bedroom for one night showed that I care for her and I'm willing to go the extra mile to help her. This is what friendship means, isn't it? The night time was our middle school dorm life all over again. At that time, we often lay on the bed, chitchatting and giggling till midnight. Though older now, we recalled our memories of those good old school days with nostalgia, amazed at how time flies. Though it was not quite cozy sleeping on the daybed, it was an enjoyable and wonderful night in her company. I'm glad I've helped others when they were in need.

亮点句型

- It was last summer when...
- People always say 'sharing means caring' and my simple act of sharing my bedroom for one night showed that...

地道表达

- reservation 预订
- due to... 由于……
- refund 退款
- high season （旅游）旺季
- stay over 住宿，过夜
- go the extra mile 加倍努力
- nostalgia 怀旧

Notes

第二节　人物类 People

1. A frequent flyer

> Describe a person who takes a plane very often.
>
> You should say:
>
> who the person is
>
> how often the person takes the plane
>
> how this affects their life
>
> and explain how you feel about this person.

思路延展

第一语组：首先明确要讲的"人物"；

第二语组：回应"坐飞机的频次"并解释原因，如工作需要、个人安排等；

第三语组：具体回应"频繁坐飞机对此人生活的影响"，多维度分层延展，如晋升、加薪等；

第四语组：核心内容，回应"你对此人的看法"，如视之为榜样等。

高分范例

The person that I would like to point out as a frequent flyer is the manager with whom I worked when I was in the internship programme at KPMG. Though he was already in his late fifties at that time, he was in charge of the audit department, which was one of the largest departments in our company. He spent a large proportion of his time working in different branches all over the world, so it was quite normal for him to be an airport goer, flying twice or more per week. He had been the platinum card member of many airlines and was often rewarded for the mileage travelled. He was primarily responsible for meeting up with clients in person, and he had to go to other cities with his team whenever a potential client turned up. His job scope also included communicating and coordinating with the heads of each branch, and updating the progress of each project through regular meetings, which was also a reason why he had to take the flights so often. He also had to report to three heads in London, New York and Beijing respectively, giving detailed presentation on the outcomes of business strategies and the performances of each branch with analytic data. Such a job made him a workaholic, working 24/7. My feelings about his lifestyle were mixed. He had been a legend in the field I worked in by earning a multimillion-dollar salary, which inspired me to climb up the hierarchy and rise to fame in the future. However, his lifestyle had also taken a heavy toll on his health, which urged me to find work-life balance rather than simply copying his unhealthy lifestyle.

亮点句型

- The person that I would like to point out as a frequent flyer is...who(m)...
- He had been a legend in the field I worked in by earning multimillion-dollar salary, which inspired me to climb up the hierarchy and rise to fame in the future.

地道表达

- internship 实习
- in charge of... 负责……
- platinum card member 铂金卡会员
- mileage travelled 飞行里程
- potential client 潜在客户
- give detailed presentation 做详细展示
- workaholic 工作狂
- take a heavy toll on... 对……造成极大伤害
- work-life balance 工作与生活的平衡

2. A person who apologises

Describe a person who has apologised to you.
You should say:
    who this person is
    when this happened
    what this person said in their apology
and explain how you felt about the apology.

思路延展

第一语组：首先明确道歉的人是谁，说明身份与关系；
第二语组：交代事情发生的时间；
第三语组：描述道歉的具体内容，包括对方所说的话、情绪、态度等；
第四语组：核心内容，重点描述自己对此事的具体感受和想法。

高分范例

I have received a lot of apologies. The one I would like to share at this moment was the one I got from Tina, my best friend who has always been a punctual person. It was a Sunday morning and we planned to watch a film together. I booked the tickets, texted her a message telling her I would pick her up at the entrance of the municipal library at 10:30 in the morning. The appointment was confirmed and then the next day, when I was there on time, she was nowhere to be found. I tried to call her but there was no answer. Since there was no parking lot there, I had to circle the area in my car. When I finally found a parking lot two miles away, I received a call back from her. She apologised profusely that she had been fully engrossed in reading, and had forgotten the time. When we arrived at the cinema, we found that the film had already started nearly a half hour earlier, and she apologised again. She said that she was extremely sorry for the trouble and inconvenience she had caused. She also said that she would do anything to make it up to me, and she begged me to name it. Then she came up with a number of choices like treating me at my favourite restaurant, buying me a cup of coffee from Starbucks, or watching another film in the evening. At that moment, I was just pretending to be angry and regretful for missing the film. I no longer felt angry because she was really sincere in her apology and she clearly valued our friendship. We watched another film and had a quality afternoon that day together.

亮点句型

- The one I would like to share at this moment was the one I got from Tina, my best friend who...
- Then she came up with a number of choices like treating me at my favourite restaurant, buying me a cup of coffee from Starbucks or watching another film in the evening.

地道表达

- a punctual person 一个准时的人
- pick her up 开车接她
- municipal library 市图书馆
- apologise profusely 连连道歉
-

3. A person who has an important job

Describe a person who has an important job.

You should say:

who the person is

what the person does

what contribution this person makes

and explain why you feel the job this person does is very important.

思路延展

第一语组：首先明确"有着重要工作的人"是谁，说明其职业、身份；

第二语组：回应"该人物的工作职责"，同时明确其职责的重要性等；

第三语组：具体回应"该人物做出的贡献"，如社会贡献、行业贡献等；

第四语组：核心内容，重点回应"该人物所做工作的重要意义"。

高分范例

Well, speaking of a person who is working in an extremely important position, I would like to single out my uncle as the ideal example. He is an attending doctor in the cardiology department of a hospital. I believe his job is crucial because he is always the key person who decides whether the patients need operations and works out the detailed plans for the operations. Therefore, he is usually under great pressure as his plan will determine the outcomes of operations, which could mean life or death to the patients. Thus, this job means huge responsibilities to bear and great courage to make tough decisions. Although he is extraordinarily experienced in this field, he has to take many uncertainties into account when making plans as the bodies and situations of various patients are quite different. He also has to prepare for some unexpected emergencies in the operating room, which could occur no matter how detailed the plan for the operation is. A good rest before the operation is essential as it is very laborious work lasting three to ten hours for any one time and he needs to be highly concentrated since he is responsible for other people's lives.

亮点句型

- Speaking of a person who..., I would like to single out...to be the ideal example.
- Therefore, he is usually under great pressure as his plan could determine the outcomes of operations, which could mean life or death to the patients.

地道表达

- cardiology department　心脏病科
- under great pressure　承受巨大压力
- outcome　结果
- take...into account　将……纳入考虑
- unexpected emergencies　意外的紧急情况
- laborious　耗时费力的
- be highly concentrated　高度集中

4. An elderly person

Describe someone who is older than you that you admire.

You should say:

　　who this person is

how you know this person

what kind of things you like to do together

and explain how you feel about this person.

思路延展

第一语组：明确要描述的人的身份，要注意一定是一个比你年长的人；

第二语组：回应"如何认识这个人的"，可以与前一语组内容合并讲述；

第三语组：列举"喜欢一起做的事情"，如做手工艺品、出游、练字等；

第四语组：核心内容，描述自己对此人的感情，重点讲述具体的感受、获得的帮助与鼓励等。

高分范例

Nobody admires my grandfather more than I do. He is creative and innovative, which can be seen in his artworks that he has made during his leisure time. Some of them are artworks for decoration such as handicrafts made of iron wires, whereas others have some practical uses, like the small baskets or pencil cases. With his bold imagination, he can always come up with designs and artifacts that could only exist in our wildest dreams. Sometimes, I have been inspired by him and have decided to make something out of my own imagination. No matter what I make, my grandfather always encourages me and proudly presents these creations to his friends. He once even organised an exhibition of all my simple artworks at home and invited many of my friends to come and view them, which has certainly boosted my self-esteem. More importantly, I've learned to think outside the box with his constant guidance and influence. I admire my grandfather and his bold imagination with all my heart.

亮点句型

● Nobody admires...more than I do.

● With his bold imagination, he can always come up with designs and artifacts that...

优质表达

● creative and innovative 富有创造性与革新精神的

● leisure time 空闲时间

● practical use 实际的应用

● come up with... 想出……，提出……

● boost 增强，提高

5. An entrepreneur

Describe a world-famous company leader.

You should say:

who the person is

how you knew this person

what quality this person has

and explain why you think this person is a good leader.

思路延展

第一语组：明确具体的"企业领导人"，细述其姓名、身份、职位等；

第二语组：回应"了解此人的途径"，如网评、新闻等；

第三语组：回应"此人所具备的品质"，可主要集中在专业、管理和领导力方面；

第四语组：核心内容，重点阐述此人的影响力及给企业带来的改变和成就。

高分范例

The inspirational leader in whom I have faith is Mark Zuckerberg. He is the independent founder of Facebook, the world-famous social media platform with over one billion users. I know of him from the comments online and the reports about him in magazines. As the leader of the company, he has talent in catering to the needs of the general public, staying competitive in the changing IT market and then standing out as an influential leader worldwide. Though I have never met him, the lists of achievement his company has achieved clearly mirror the competency of the leader who is managing the company. Undoubtedly, his mastery of the cutting-edge software technology and the leadership he offers in making the right decisions during tough situations leads the company to success. Plus, he is extremely influential among the young people. His emphasis on integrity, dedication to charity, and deep concerns about the underprivileged in society all add up to his leadership being significant for the younger generation, which is also why I have faith in his leadership. Finally, I do believe he is the one who can take the lead in the future in other ways as he is energetic, full of inspiration and, most importantly, he is a man who dreams and has the courage to realise his dreams. This is the quality that matters most for being a leader.

亮点句型

● The inspirational leader in whom I have faith is...

● As the leader of the company, he has talent in catering to the needs of the general public, staying competitive in the changing IT market and then standing out as an influential leader worldwide.

- His emphasis on integrity, dedication to charity, and deep concerns about the underprivileged in society all add up to his leadership being significant for the younger generation, which is also why I have faith in his leadership.

地道表达

- have faith in...　相信……，信任……
- cater to...　迎合……，满足……
- stand out　引人注目
- mirror　反映出
- cutting edge　尖端的，前沿的
- the underprivileged　弱势群体

Notes

第三节 事件类 Events

1. A crowded activity

Describe a really crowded activity you have attended.

You should say:

    what the activity was

    when and where the activity was held

    what you did there

and explain how you felt about the crowded activity.

思路延展

第一语组：明确具体的"活动"，交代具体的活动背景与场景信息；

第二语组：回应"活动的时间和地点"，可拓展论述地点的重要性、选择的原因等；

第三语组：回应具体的"活动内容"，可涉及活动细节、获得的好处、所见所闻等；

第四语组：重点回应"自己对这种拥挤活动的感受与体验"。

高分范例

Well, that's an interesting question and I would like to share a recent experience of mine. I went to the annual food festival with a group of friends in Sydney last month, which was held by the government and tourism board, lasting 12 days. It was located at a park near Darling Harbour, covering thousands of square metres. It attracted chefs and restaurants of various cultures from tens of countries that set up booths there, catering to thousands of eaters and tourists each day. Helpers for each booth carefully manoeuvred in the crowded streets, offering food samples for visitors to try. We were in the huge crowds, seeing countless people trying the delicious foods, and admiring the diverse food cultures while taking pictures. Everyone was laughing and shouting excitedly, enjoying their time there. My feeling towards this crowded activity was a little complicated. On one hand, I was happy to be there because I had the chance to try something new and fresh at a relatively lower price while having a great time with my friends. On the other hand, I was a bit worried that the boisterous crowd might lead to a stampede, which put me off from staying there for too long.

亮点句型

- I went to the annual food festival with a group of friends in Sydney last month, which was held by the government and tourism board, lasting 12 days.

地道表达

- the annual food festival　年度美食节
- tourism board　旅游局
- cover thousands of square metres　覆盖几千平方米
- tens of countries　几十个国家
- set up a booth　设展位
- at a relatively lower price　以相对较低的价格
- stampede　踩踏事件

2. A good service you received

Describe a good service you received.

You should say:

　　when and where it happened

　　what situation you were in

　　how you were served

and how you felt about the service.

思路延展

第一语组：首先给出事件发生的具体时间、地点等信息；

第二语组：描述事件发生的情景，介绍细节并且描述过程；

第三语组：回应"如何被服务"，描述具体的服务细节以及这一服务是如何超越期待的等；

第四语组：重点回应"对此服务的感受"，讲述自己的体验和感想等。

高分范例

The time when I received very good service was extremely memorable. It was last summer when I took a trip with my family to Shanghai to visit the newly opened Disney Land. We booked a room in the Sheraton Hotel near our destination. Unfortunately, when we were about to check in at the front desk, the staff told me that there was no such a reservation. I checked my app immediately, finding that my booking had been cancelled without any prior notice due to unstable Internet signal. To make it worse, all the rooms were already fully booked and occupied and such was the situation at most of the hotels nearby, and we were left in an awkward situation with nowhere to stay that night. Although it was mostly the fault of my carelessness, the staff in the hotel made great efforts to help us. The receptionist called all the hotels nearby, asking whether they could offer a room at the same price. After about 30 minutes she successfully helped us get a room in another hotel, which was just three kilometres away. Then she arranged hotel porters to help carry our luggage and book a taxi, which saved us tons of trouble. When she shook hands with us and thanked us for choosing their hotel, I was extremely touched and told her I would definitely reserve their hotel next time I came to Shanghai. This experience well reflected the high-quality service of the hotel, and their taking responsibility for every guest in every detail. Thus, I was really impressed.

亮点句型

- Although it was mostly the fault of my carelessness, the staff in the hotel made great efforts to help us.

地道表达

- front desk　前台
- without prior notice　没提前通知
- to make it worse　更糟糕的是
- awkward　难处理的
- make great efforts to do sth.　努力做某事
- hotel porter　酒店行李员

3. A happy family event

Describe a happy family event from your childhood that you remember well.

You should say:

　　what the event is

　　when and where it happened

　　what you saw or did

and explain why you remember this event so well.

思路延展

第一语组：首先明确具体的"家庭活动"回应主题，与提纲中的 what the event is 结合并强调 happy；

第二语组：回应"活动的时间和地点"，可与活动内容相结合；

第三语组：回应"看到什么或做了什么"，描述活动过程；

第四语组：重点回应"为什么对这一活动记忆深刻"，可讲述其激励作用、对学习兴趣的培养等。

高分范例

Of the many fascinating memories I have from family events and moments in the childhood, I would like to talk about the riddle guessing event my family and I attended each year. It took place during the Lantern Festival, which was at the end of the Spring Festival. On that special day, the streets near our neighbourhood would be decorated with intricate lanterns infused with traditional Chinese elements, and all the riddles were hung on the lanterns. We would enjoy the views of lanterns while collecting the riddles. The questions were updated every year so it was quite hard to get them all right. The content of the riddles covered a wide range of fields, from the names of certain objects to some concepts in geography or astronomy, and thus, the riddles were extremely challenging. We usually held interesting in-family competitions and set some awards for the winners. The person who got six questions correct would be the winner and got a souvenir. Sometimes, my parents set a small amount of money as prizes as well to encourage my cousins and me to guess more riddles. It was one of the most meaningful events in my childhood and I always tried my best to get some extra pocket money. Besides, it was intellectually stimulating, encouraging me to read more books and broaden my knowledge so that I could be the winner the following year.

亮点句型

- Of the many fascinating memories I have from the family events and moments in the childhood, I would like to talk about the riddle guessing event my family and I attended each year.
- The content of the riddles covered a wide range of fields, from the names of certain objects to some concepts in geography or astronomy...

地道表达

- fascinating memory　迷人的回忆
- riddle　谜语
- the Lantern Festival　元宵节
- infuse with...　注入……
- a wide range of...　范围广泛的……
- pocket money　零花钱

4. A mistake

Describe a mistake you have ever made.

You should say:

　　what it was about

　　when and where it happened

　　why you had to apologise

and explain what you have learnt from the mistake.

思路延展

第一语组：首先明确"犯过的错"，回应主题；

第二语组：回应"发生的时间与地点"，描述事情经过；

第三语组：结合具体的错误回应"要道歉的原因"；

第四语组：重点回应"从这次犯错事件中学到的东西"，可拓展到责任感、担当等。

高分范例

Speaking of mistakes I have made, I remember that I misunderstood a good person when I was a sophomore in college. That was unforgettable, and I apologised and was forgiven thereafter. The story went like this. One day, I just could not find my necklace in my dorm, though I remembered I had left it on my desk the night before. I searched every corner but it was nowhere to be found. When I became increasingly frustrated, I began to suspect that one of my roommates, Tina, who had just had a fight with me the night before, deliberately hid it or even threw it away to get back at me. I was convinced about my unfounded speculation, and secretly spread rumours about how she had been stealing valuables from others. The rumour spread fast and many students accused her when their belongings went missing. However, everything changed when it turned out that I had actually left my necklace in the pocket of my coat at home and I realised how unfairly I had treated Tina. Therefore, I apologised sincerely. I wrote an open letter, informing everyone of her innocence and I gave my sincere apology, saying sorry in front of her and all my classmates. Tina forgave me, so I made up with her and we became good friends. This taught me that we should not judge others when we make thing up, or use false deduction or doubts. Moreover, taking responsibility for what you've done wrong is a good thing.

亮点句型

- When I became increasingly frustrated, I began to doubt that one of my roommates, Tina, who had just had a fight with me the night before, deliberately hid it or even threw it away to get back at me.

地道表达

- deliberately　蓄意地
- get back at sb.　报复某人
- unfounded speculation　毫无根据的猜测
- spread rumours　传播谣言
- accuse　指控
- make up with sb.　与某人和解

5. A special meal

Describe a special meal or a picnic you had with friends.

You should say:

　　when and where you ate with your friends

what you ate and drank

why you ate together

and explain what made the meal special.

思路延展

第一语组：明确具体的聚餐活动，包括时间、地点等相关信息；

第二语组：进行具体的餐食描述，可与活动情景、意义、目的等相结合；

第三语组：具体回应"一起吃饭的原因"，如娱乐放松、增进友谊等；

第四语组：重点回应"这次聚餐的意义"。

高分范例

The most special meal I have ever had was a barbecue I had with my friends last year. It was a sunny day and my friend Lily was about to leave for the US to pursue her Master's degree. Prior to her departure, I planned this personalised barbecue as a surprise farewell gift. Even though I had never set foot in the kitchen before, I was determined to take the role of chef this time. There were several highlights worth mentioning. It was held in the garden where we usually hung out when we were young. It was a place full of memories, and that was why we had chosen this site for the barbecue. I spent days preparing for this special event, purchasing food ingredients, trying out the cuisine and designing the menu. Then came the most difficult part, the barbecue sauce, since I always failed to get the flavour I wanted. After trying several times, I managed to get the right flavour. On the actual day, everything went smoothly. I got all the equipment settled at the garden while my friends helped arrange the table. It turned out that I was quite a talented cook, and the flavour went beyond our expectations. We sat on the picnic blanket, relaxing while chatting about our plans for the future. Even now, this scene is still very clear in my memory.

亮点句型

● Prior to her departure, I planned this personalised barbecue as a surprise farewell gift.

● Even though I had never set foot in the kitchen before, I was determined to take the role of chef this time.

● It was held in the garden where we usually hung out when we were young.

地道表达

● be about to do sth.　正准备做某事

● leave for...　前往……

● Master's degree　硕士学位

● prior to...　在……之前

● set foot in...　涉足……

● take the role of...　扮演……的角色

● hang out　闲逛

● turn out　结果是

- beyond one's expectation   *超出某人的期待*

6. A trip

Describe a trip to the place near water.

You should say:

where it was

who you went with

what you did

and explain why it was a memorable experience.

思路延展

第一语组：首先明确"去哪里旅行"，回应主题；

第二语组：回应"同去的人"，可以结合"出行的目的"叙述；

第三语组：回应"具体做的事情"，同时与当地特点结合；

第四语组：重点回应"难忘的原因"，如此行的意义、收获等。

高分范例

I would like to share about my trip to Qingdao, a coastal city. I went there with a bunch of friends and we decided to join a fund-raising activity that required us to cycle in the city to gather more support from the general public. This activity was named after a charitable organisation that planned to sponsor the renovation of various historical heritage sites in the city. We mapped out the routes so that we could have a quality time travelling along the seaside while also raising money for a good cause. We cycled in a row, with flags that promoted the charitable activities flapping behind us. During the ride, we breathed in the salty fresh air, talking and singing, and stopped once to have a picnic at lunch time. We cycled nearly 50 miles that day and a lot of interesting things happened along the way. The trip was pretty impressive because we did something meaningful for this beautiful city, and we indeed had a great time there.

亮点句型

- We mapped out the routes so that we could have a quality time travelling along the seaside while also raising money for a good cause.

地道表达

- fund-raising activity   *筹款活动*
- name after...   *以……命名*
- charitable organisation   *慈善机构*
- sponsor   *赞助*

- map out the routes   规划路线
- raise money for a good cause   为公益事业筹集资金

7. An experience

Describe an experience that has changed your life.

You should say:

what this change was

how it happened

where it happened

and explain why it changed your life in a positive way.

思路延展

第一语组：明确具体"经历的事件"，如蹦极，并且结合"自己的改变"来回应主题；

第二语组：回应"具体发生的过程"，体现出对事件的叙述能力；

第三语组：具体回应"事件的地点"，结合前面讲的"如何发生"进行细化解释；

第四语组：重点回应"对你的生活产生了怎样的积极影响"，可延伸到对自己的性格、态度的影响等。

高分范例

The experience that has totally changed the way I look at myself was bungee jumping in Kawarau Bridge in New Zealand. I was once a shy girl when I was in high school. At that time, I often doubted myself for no reason. However, when I went to this place famous for bungee jumping in New Zealand, I was encouraged to try this extreme sport. I had no idea what I was getting myself into, so I agreed without thinking twice. When I stood at the top of the mountain, looking down at the river hundreds of metres below, I deeply regretted making this decision. I couldn't bring myself to look down for a second longer, let alone jump right over. My friends who had already tried the sport shouted out to me how excited they were and how memorable the experience could be. Standing at the edge of the platform with a bunch of friends cheering me on, I knew there was no way back and I had to jump. Their encouragement gave me the courage to finally take the step. I closed my eyes and forced myself to jump. As wind was rushing all around me and roaring in my ears, I did not experience any excitement but there wasn't fear either. All difficulties and dangerous possibilities were just unnecessary figments of my imagination built out of fear. I realised that if I could overcome the unnecessary fears, I could accomplish anything with a willing heart. From then on, I just believe in trying and I encourage myself to make efforts rather than just think negatively. I'll never know what I can do until I try after all. That experience has totally changed the way I think and the person I am today.

亮点句型

- The experience that has totally changed the way I look at myself was bungee jumping in Kawarau Bridge in New Zealand.
- I had no idea what I was getting myself into, so I agreed without thinking twice.

地道表达

- for no reason 毫无理由
- get sb. into... 使某人陷入……
- cheer sb. on 为某人加油
- from then on 自那之后

8. Sky watching

Describe a time in which you watched the sky.

You should say:

    when this happened

    who you were with

    what you saw

and explain how you felt about watching the sky.

思路延展

第一语组：明确具体的"时刻"，以先铺垫后强调的方式讲出本次事件为何值得谈论；

第二语组：回应"一起看天的人"，细化并描述相关的背景；

第三语组：回应"看到了什么"，描述具体的场景；

第四语组：回应"当时的感受"，比如描述面对壮观景象时自己的心情、美好的回忆以及重要的意义等。

高分范例

Well, my friends and I like to watch the sky when the weather is fine. As air pollution has been under control lately, the air is so clear that we can observe the starry night just with our eyes. Sometimes, I also use my astronomical telescope to observe constellations more clearly. There was a time when my friends and I watched the sky for nearly a whole night last year, although I can't remember the specific date. The Meteorological Station said that there would be a meteor shower from Leo that night and that a person could observe it in the urban areas with the naked eye. This once in a life time experience attracted thousands of citizens to join sky watching groups and some companies turned off the decoration lights on their office buildings to reduce light pollution. Though it was a little cold outside, we were so thrilled and filled with excitement that the chilly air did not even bother us. We stared at the starry night patiently and finally at midnight, a meteor strode through the sky, and then another one, and then meteors showered down like a grand fireworks display. It was the first time I had witnessed a scene so magnificent, leaving me staring at the sky in awe. We did not sleep that night at all, but the waiting was worth it.

亮点句型

- As air pollution has been under control lately, the air is so clear that we can observe the starry night just with our eyes.
- There was a time when my friends and I watched the sky for nearly a whole night last year, although I can't remember the specific date.

地道表达

- under control 得到控制
- astronomical telescope 天文望远镜
- constellation 星座
- Meteorological Station 气象站
- meteor shower 流星雨
- Leo 狮子座
- the naked eye 肉眼
- light pollution 光污染
- thrilled 极为激动的
- magnificent 壮丽的，宏伟的
- in awe 敬畏地

9. Something you ate

Describe something you ate for the first time.

You should say:

what it was

when you ate it

why you ate it

and explain how you felt about it.

思路延展

第一语组：明确具体的事件，即"第一次吃某种食物"，回应主题；

第二语组：回应事件发生的时间，可以联系某个特殊的时刻以赋予该事件意义；

第三语组：回应"第一次尝试的原因"，如该食物的吸引力、别人的推荐等；

第四语组：重点回应"自己的感受"，可从多个层面阐述这件事的意义。

The specific food that I would like to talk about in more detail at this moment, which impressed me the very first time, would be the hamburger at KFC. This answer popped right into my mind when I was reading the question. It was a Sunday afternoon during my summer vacation that I went to KFC for the very first time. The first KFC was just introduced to my hometown, and my father treated me so that I could try the exotic and unique American cuisine which he believed was extremely rich in flavour. The other reason was that my father wanted to celebrate my great improvement in academic performance on the mid-term examination that day. I can clearly remember the feeling at that time. Firstly, the hamburgers looked weird and tasted a little too spicy. Even so, I still tried two hamburgers. Secondly, I was touched by the thoughtfulness of my father, and I could feel his love and care behind his unspoken encouragement. Finally, I started to feel the cultural gap between Eastern and Western culture, which was fascinating. These differences stimulated my interest in foreign cultures and drove me to read more and learn more about these cultures.

亮点句型

- It was a Sunday afternoon during my summer vacation that I went to KFC for the very first time.

地道表达

- pop into one's mind　某人的脑海中立即浮现
- treat sb.　请某人吃饭
- academic performance　学业成绩
- mid-term　期中的
- weird　奇特的
- spicy　辣的
- be touched by...　被……感动
- cultural gap　文化差异

10. Something you have waited for

Describe something you have waited for.

You should say:

what it was

who waited with you

why you had to wait

and explain how you felt when waiting.

第一语组：明确"等待的事情"，同时交代时间、地点等信息；

第二语组：回应"一起等待的人"，无论是独自一人还是与朋友一起都要交代清楚；

第三语组：回应"等待的原因"，可一并描述等待的经过；

第四语组：重点回应"等待的感受"，可在描述"等待的经过"的同时讲感受。

高分范例

I have waited for something many times before, and the one I would like to talk about at this time is when I waited for the 4D *Harry Potter* film with my friends. I went to Japan with my friends by plane, and we planned to watch the film at Universal Studios there. The cinema was located at the centre of the Harry Potter theme park. We had to wait there for a long time because thousands of visitors were queuing for the film. The theme park was newly built and it was extremely popular among young people. We decided to wait patiently because the main purpose of our visiting Universal Studios, and even Japan, was watching this film and visiting this theme park. The film was also exclusive to the Japanese Universal Studios, and hence, it would be such a pity if we missed it. I should say we had a lot of fun watching it and the time spent waiting was definitely worthwhile. We had a wonderful time discussing and sharing insights about *Harry Potter* while waiting together, and the few hours of waiting passed surprisingly fast. We even made friends with some of the visitors, so I would say the waiting time was not that unbearable and even kind of enjoyable.

亮点句型

- I have waited for something many times before, and the one I would like to talk about at this time is my waiting for a 4D film of *Harry Potter* with my friends.

地道表达

- Universal Studios　环球影城
- theme park　主题公园
- exclusive　独有的
- definitely worthwhile　绝对值得
- share insights　分享见解

11. To be polite

Describe a situation in which you had to be polite.

You should say:

　　when and what situation you were in

　　why you had to be polite

　　how you did it

and explain your feeling about this situation.

思路延展

第一语组：首先明确具体的"情景"，回应主题，说明事件发生的时间、地点等情况；

第二语组：回应"需要礼貌的具体原因"，与情景中的要求相结合，说明必要性；

第三语组：具体回应"如何做的"，描述细节；

第四语组：重点回应"自己的感受"，可描述由此获得的体验、感受等。

高分范例

Well, though I am always a good-mannered person, there was once a situation in which I had to be extremely polite by request. There was a time when I volunteered as a tour guide and interpreter at the Shanghai World Expo for nearly a whole summer. I guided the visitors around the exhibition in the Expo, giving them simple descriptions and explanations in standard English and answering all their questions patiently. The speed and tone of my speaking as well as my gestures and postures were all trained to follow strict standards so that I could be as polite and respectful towards the visitors as possible. Whenever foreign friends visited, I would ask them politely if they needed a tour guide to explain the cultures, themes and significance of the exhibition in English. Most of them would gladly say yes, and then I would show them around the exhibition hall, trying to pronounce every word as clearly as possible. Even though I could not explain some parts that were too complex or too abstract, all the tourists were very understanding and considerate, encouraging me along the way whenever I became overly nervous. I treated every tourist as politely as possible because I knew clearly that I was representing our nation and our culture. It was definitely a very rewarding experience for me. I was firstly well trained in behaviour and diction in every detail, which would benefit me in the future. More importantly, I really felt the power behind politeness, which helps people from different cultural backgrounds communicate pleasantly.

亮点句型

● Though I am always a good-mannered person, there was once a situation in which...

● There was a time when...

● Whenever foreign friends visited, I would ask them politely if they need...

地道表达

● good mannered person　有教养的人

● volunteer as...　志愿担任……

● Shanghai World Expo　上海世博会

● understanding and considerate　善解人意的，体贴的

● behaviour and diction　言行举止

12. To get up early

Describe a time you got up extremely early.

You should say:

when this happened

what you needed to do that day

what time you got up

and explain how you felt about getting up that early on that day.

思路延展

第一语组：首先明确"一次早起的经历"，如观看升旗仪式等，提供活动的时间信息；

第二语组：回应"要做的事情"，同时阐述早起的原因；

第三语组：回应"需要早起的精准时间"，同时描述自己早起时的状态，如疲惫、兴奋等；

第四语组：重点回应"对这次早起事件的感受"，如带来的收获、事件本身的意义等。

高分范例

As to an experience of getting up early, I would like to talk about the one when my friends and I watched the flag-raising ceremony in Beijing last year. We visited Beijing for just one week during our summer vacation, and we decided to spend a Tuesday morning observing the whole flag-raising ceremony on Tian'anmen Square. In order to watch the entire ceremony, we had to get up quite early at 4 am. Though the ceremony started at 6 am, we had to allow sufficient time to get dressed and travel from our hostel to Tian'anmen Square which would take nearly 50 minutes. Rather than having gone to bed early, we stayed up late talking and playing cards until 2 in the morning, too excited to fall asleep. However, I did not feel tired when we got up at 4 am, eager to witness the solemn ceremony with my own eyes. All the trouble we went through to watch the flag-raising ceremony was definitely worthwhile. When I watched the rising national flag begin to gently flap in the summer breeze and heard thousands of people coming to watch the ceremony sing the national anthem with passion and awe, I felt a sense of belonging that I had never felt so strongly before. At that moment I was determined to work harder so that I could better serve this place that I will always call home. Thanks to this experience of getting up early, I had such a memorable morning.

亮点句型

- As to an experience of getting up early, I would like to talk about the one when my friends and I watched the flag-raising ceremony in Beijing last year.

- Rather than having gone to bed early, we stayed up late talking and playing cards until 2 in the morning, too excited to fall asleep.

- flag-raising ceremony　升旗仪式
- national anthem　国歌
- allow sufficient time　留出足够的时间
- passion and awe　热爱与敬畏
- witness　目睹

13. To speak in a foreign language

Describe a time when you first spoke in a foreign language.

You should say:

　　where and when it happened

　　who you spoke to

　　what you spoke about

and explain how you felt about the conversation.

思路延展

第一语组：明确"讲外语的时间和地点"，交代事件的背景；

第二语组：回应"交谈的对象"，叙述事件的过程；

第三语组：回应"谈话的内容"，描述此过程中的心理变化及面对的挑战等；

第四语组：重点回应"对这次谈话的感受"，可讨论从中获得的成就感以及对自己以后生活的影响等。

高分范例

As to my very first time speaking a foreign language, it was unforgettable and quite encouraging. It took place on a plane to South Korea, when I was in primary school. When I was a fourth grader, my parents took me to South Korea on a trip. My English was rather poor then, and I was afraid of speaking even a single word in English. During the flight, I told my father what I would like to buy and where to visit. To my surprise, my father agreed to my arrangements, on the condition that I spoke English as much as possible, like making inquiries, asking for prices and bargaining, or booking the hotels, etc. The first task my father gave me was to talk to the stewardess and ask for a drink for my father. I practised the simple sentence of asking for a cup of coffee many times, with my heart beating faster and faster. Finally, I screwed up my courage and managed to say some words out loud. To my surprise, the stewardess understood what I meant and she talked to me in simple English with an accent. I breathed a sigh of relief as my request expressed in English had been understood. I was so excited that I forgot about my anxiety. We even chatted for a while in English and I realised that my English was not as poor as I had imagined. Language is a communication tool. The more I use it, the better I master it. During that trip, I talked with Korean people in English as much as possible, with gestures, yet had some occasional embarrassing misunderstandings, though. But it was fun, and I enjoyed the trip. Since then I have been more confident in my English and have begun to use English more often.

亮点句型

- As to my very first time speaking a foreign language, it was unforgettable and quite encouraging.
- I was so excited that I forgot about my anxiety.

地道表达

- unforgettable 难以忘怀的
- primary school 小学
- on the condition that 条件是
- make inquiries 询问

- stewardess （飞机上的）女乘务员
- screw up the courage 鼓足勇气
- breathe a sigh of relief 松了口气

14. To use your imagination

Describe a time when you needed to use your imagination.

You should say:

what the situation was

why you needed to use your imagination

what difficulties there were

and explain how you felt about it.

思路延展

第一语组：明确具体的"情形"，回应活动类型、名称等细节；

第二语组：回应"需要使用想象力的原因"，描述该活动的特征；

第三语组：具体回应"面对的困难"，可从多方面进行描述；

第四语组：重点回应"对此感受如何"，可论述对自己来说比较有意思的方面，阐述活动的意义等。

高分范例

There have been many occasions in which I have had to use my imagination, and I would like to talk about a time that required me to think outside the box. I attended a competition named Guess It. In the game, we were divided into several groups and I had to guess what my teammate had read based on her body movements. The quicker I guessed the answer, the higher our scores would be. We also had to rotate the roles and then I would be the one to act out the words or idioms I saw. The difficulties were that when I was guessing, I had to imagine tons of scenarios that were potentially related to the action my teammate did, and then shout out words that were associated with the scenarios one by one. The most challenging part was to come up with the right words. For example, when my teammate did a motion that seemed to be sweeping the floor, I shouted out all the words that were even only loosely connected to sweeping, from 'broom' to 'detergent', while the correct answer was 'cleaner'. The overall experience was hilarious, with people totally misreading their partners' actions. I believe this experience clearly highlights the importance of the ability to imagine. The top scores in this game were by those who were able to let their imagination go wild, coming up with tens of related words and thus having a higher chance of guessing the exact correct words.

亮点句型

- There have been many occasions in which I have had to use my imagination, and I would like to talk about a time that required me to think outside the box.
- The quicker I guessed the answer, the higher our scores would be.

地道表达

- think outside the box　突破思维定式
- tons of...　大量……，很多……
- scenario　设想
- come up with　想出，提出
- hilarious　欢闹的，滑稽的
- misread　误解
- highlight the importance　强调重要性
- let one's imagination go wild　让某人的想象力尽情发挥

Notes

第四节　描述类 Description

1. A choice

Describe a choice that troubled you ever so much.

You should say:

    what choice it was

    how this choice troubled you

    how you made the decision

and explain what you felt about this decision.

思路延展

第一语组：明确具体的"选择"，交代事件背景等信息；

第二语组：回应"让自己感到麻烦的方面"，分别论述各个方面的影响及优劣势；

第三语组：具体回应"做决定的过程及相关问题"，如需要付出的成本、代价等；

第四语组：回应"对此决定的感受"。

高分范例

There was once a tough decision-making process that tortured me for months. I was faced with the choice of whether or not I should grab the chance to study in Germany for one year, since I was qualified for the exchange programme funded by the government last year. I was keen to study abroad, meeting professors and schoolmates from various cultural backgrounds and gaining more insights. However, the practical problems that I had to tackle made me think twice. Though this programme was entirely funded by the government, it was the very first year of the programme, and hence many issues hadn't been settled between my college and the college in Germany, such as my credit transfer. The credits I would earn in Germany could not be transferred back to my college in China, which meant I would have to postpone my graduation when I came back. Or otherwise, I would have to burn too much midnight oil and hit the books cramming on the nights before exams if I still wanted to graduate on time. This sounded intimidating but it would also be a challenge that would push me forward. Besides, I would have to work part time through college since I did not want my parents to pay the hefty living expenses abroad. I turned to my teachers and friends for advice and they offered me their points of view. My parents told me that they could pay some of the expenses to alleviate some stress for me, but I declined their kind offer since I was already an adult then and felt I had to shoulder my own responsibilities. I finally listed out all the pros and cons, rethinking the benefits and drawbacks. Thereafter, I clearly knew what to do. I rejected the offer and felt relieved.

亮点句型

- There was once a tough decision-making process that tortured me for months.
- I was faced with the choice of whether or not I should grab the chance to study in Germany for one year, since I was qualified for the exchange programme funded by the government last year.

地道表达

- grab the chance 抓住机会
- be qualified for... 有……的资格
- tackle 应对，解决
- credit 学分
- burn the midnight oil 学习或工作到深夜

- hit the books 用功学习
- cram （为应考）临时死记硬背
- sound intimidating 听起来很吓人
- hefty living expenses 昂贵的生活费
- feel relieved 感到释然

2. A class

Describe a class or training session that you enjoyed.

You should say:

　　what the teacher did

　　when and where you had this class or training session

　　what you learned in this class or training session

and explain why you enjoyed it.

思路延展

第一语组：首先明确具体的"课程或训练项目"；

第二语组：回应"老师的作用""具体时间和地点"等细节问题；

第三语组：具体回应"比较有收获感的内容"；

第四语组：核心内容，重点论述"自己为什么喜欢这一课程或训练项目"。

Well, I joined a training seminar named 'Be the Owner of Your Time', featuring some important skills for time management. In class, the lecturer first introduced some theories on how to divide one's free time into different tasks. This informative class was held in a business school in Qingdao for two weekends, which really helped me become a more organised person. The lecturer pointed out the common problem we have when managing our time which is spending too much time on urgent but not important things, leaving important tasks undone. The lecturer explained how to draw up a schedule according to the order of priority, focusing on completing important but not urgent tasks first. Now grading the urgency of each issue has become a part of my routine. I enjoyed this seminar, through which I have gained deeper insights into time management, and learned to achieve work-life balance. Finally, this programme helped me get rid of the bad habit of procrastination since I now know what needs to be done quickly and can act in a timely fashion.

亮点句型

- I joined a training seminar named 'Be the Owner of Your Time', featuring some important skills for time management.

地道表达

- training seminar　研修班
- feature　以……为特色
- schedule　日程安排

- order of priority　轻重缓急次序
- procrastination　拖延

3. A film about the future

Describe a film about the future.

You should say:

what it is

what the film is about

what is special about it

and explain why it attracted you.

思路延展

第一语组：首先明确具体的"影片"名称；

第二语组：描述这部电影的大概内容；

第三语组：描述电影的具体情节以及特别之处，重点结合与"未来"相关的信息；

第四语组：论述这部电影的吸引人之处，可从故事的真实性、寓意，以及看完电影的感受等方面阐述。

高分范例

As for my favourite future-themed film, I'd like to talk about the one named *The Day After Tomorrow*, which is about the disastrous consequences brought about by global warming. The story goes like this. A meteorologist, the leading actor in the film, detects unusual changes in the world's climate and reports his findings to the government. However, no one takes him seriously, just like how every film of this kind goes at the beginning. One day a terrible snowstorm strikes New York City and the temperature plummets to the extent that humans could freeze to death outdoors. The film portrays survivors who manage to find refuge at a library but who struggle to live with an extreme shortage of fuel and medical supplies. Although it is just a typical Hollywood blockbuster, I was still deeply moved by the humanitarian values and resilience all people upheld in the face of this great disaster for mankind. The film also acts as a warning for us. If we don't take measures to protect our environment right now, maybe in the near future, all those scenes depicted in the film may become real. Another thing I liked it about were the special effects used to heighten the stifling and helpless atmosphere. In sharp contrast to the devastating effects of this long-lasting snowstorm, human beings are vulnerable and insignificant in the face of nature. Though the same theme and plot have been used over and over again in other films with only minor twists, it has been the benchmark in this kind of film and has not been overtaken so far.

亮点句型

● As for my favourite future-themed film, I'd like to talk about..., which is about...
● It has been the benchmark in this kind of film and has not been overtaken so far.

地道表达

● future-themed　以未来为主题的
● global warming　全球变暖
● meteorologist　气象学家
● take...seriously　认真对待……
● plummet　暴跌，速降

● blockbuster　轰动一时的大作
● take measures　采取措施
● sharp contrast　鲜明对比
● benchmark　标杆，赶超目标

4. A foreign food

Describe a foreign food you have had.

You should say:

　　when you ate it

where you got it

what you actually ate

and explain how you felt while eating such food.

思路延展

第一语组：明确具体的"食物"名称（平时要注意积累与食物相关的词汇）和吃到该食物的时间；

第二语组：继续回应"地点"，讲述吃到该食物的情形，可具体到某个街道或某家餐厅；

第三语组：具体回应"吃了什么"，可描述该食物的构成、食材、做法以及自己对这种食物的期待、想要品尝的原因等；

第四语组：重点回应"品尝该食物的感受"，可详细描述食物的美味、背后的文化等。

高分范例

I would like to say something about the sushi I ate while travelling in Tokyo, Japan. I tried this food in an ordinary restaurant one night because I really wanted to taste common Japanese food that local Japanese had on a daily basis. I went to a small-sized sushi bar which could merely hold a dozen customers. Delicate porcelain plates with sushi were put on a conveyor belt which went around the dining tables, and I could take any plates with sushi that attracted me. Most of the sushi was made of rice and raw fish or other seafood. I tried some with salmon and tuna, and some with seafood even though I had no idea what it was. Nonetheless, it was an enjoyable eating experience overall. The food was carefully prepared and tasty, and this traditional Japanese food offered me more insight into Japanese culture. What surprised me most was the mustard sauce, and I totally fell in love with this spicy yet addictive sauce. With a cup of sake, I felt really relaxed in this tiny Japanese restaurant. Though I did not go to those more famous diners, which were extremely expensive and even required appointments a few months in advance, I was impressed by the quality food the sushi bar offered.

亮点句型

● I went to a small-sized sushi bar which could merely hold a dozen customers.

地道表达

● sushi bar   寿司店
● a dozen   一打
● conveyor belt   传送带

● raw fish   生鱼片
● addictive   使人上瘾的
● sake   日本清酒

5. A game or sport

Describe a game or sport you enjoy playing.

You should say:

    what kind of game or sport it is

    who you play it with

    where you play it

and explain why you enjoy playing it.

思路延展

第一语组：首先明确具体的"运动或比赛项目"，说明其形式与意义；

第二语组：回应"一起运动的人"，可适当说明运动规则、人数等；

第三语组：回应"运动的地点"，明确场地及设备要求等；

第四语组：重点回应"喜欢这项运动的原因"，如有利于健康、培养团队精神、锻炼意志力等。

高分范例

The sport I'm particularly keen on and would like to talk about in more detail at this moment is soccer. I will never get tired of this sport, and nothing can bring me more joy, vitality and confidence than this sport. This sport is played worldwide, with millions of crazy fans. We have inter-school, inter-city and nation-wide games as well as the World Cup and the European Cup, and here in China, we have CSL and many more. I play this game with many different people, like teammates in school, playmates in the community, or other teams we meet when playing in the school playgrounds. I go to various places to play soccer in addition to the fixed places where I am routinely trained, such as the sports stadium or the school playgrounds of many different campuses. Sometimes, I even go to other cities to play to get more experience. I am so fond of this sport for several reasons. Firstly, it can rejuvenate me and release my stress when I play soccer. Secondly, I feel a sense of accomplishment when I score a goal, especially when I help my team win the game. Plus, I am able to make a lot of friends whenever my teammates and I play against other teams. Soccer has changed me both physically and mentally. I will strive to keep fit while upholding the unyielding spirit of soccer players.

亮点句型

- The sport I'm particularly keen on and would like to talk about in more detail at this moment is soccer.
- I will never get tired of this sport, and nothing can bring me more joy, vitality and confidence than this sport.

地道表达

- get tired of... 厌烦……
- nation-wide 全国范围的
- rejuvenate 使精力充沛
- score a goal 进球得分
- unyielding spirit 不屈的精神

6. A historical period

Describe a historical period that you are interested in.

You should say:

what the historical period is

how you know it

what happened during that period

and explain why you find it interesting.

思路延展

第一语组：明确具体的"历史时期"，讲出朝代及相关信息；

第二语组：回应"如何了解到这段历史"，如通过书籍、文章、画作、影视作品等；

第三语组：具体回应"此时期发生的事情"，结合了解的途径对事件进行描述；

第四语组：重点回应"觉得此历史时期有意思的原因"，可描述从中获得的信息、知识与感受等。

高分范例

The period that I want to talk about is a very prosperous period in China, the North Song Dynasty. I got to know this period from history classes first, which did not capture my interest at all at that time. However, from the moment I saw the Chinese traditional painting named *Life Along the Bian River at the Pure Brightness Festival*, one of the top ten renowned paintings in the world, I fell in love with the rich and diverse culture during the North Song Dynasty depicted in the painting. From the painting I could see how the people of different classes in the period lived, which prompted me to read more books and browse more websites, getting to know the significant events and famous people at that time. There were various forms of art in that period and the social economy developed extremely fast, way ahead of other countries during that period, so that people could express themselves through paintings and poems without constrains. Architecture with exotic elements became the trading places in the capital while countless stalls opened along the street with sales people calling out to attract potential customers. The reason why I found it interesting was that when I observed the painting, I was instantaneously attracted to the landscape of the capital, people's clothing and the lifestyle represented in the painting. I visited the same spot depicted in the painting last year, and I was deeply amazed by how the capital with a long history has developed into a steel and concrete city dominated by skyscrapers. This allows me to gain insight into Chinese history in depth.

亮点句型

- The period that I want to talk about is a very prosperous period in China, the North Song Dynasty.
- There were various forms of art in that period and the social economy developed extremely fast, way ahead of other countries during that period, so that people could express themselves through paintings and poems without constrains.

地道表达

- prosperous period 繁荣的时期
- capture my interest 吸引我的注意力
- instantaneously 即刻
- gain insight into... 深入理解……

7. A noise

Describe a noise that bothers you.

You should say:

what it is and where it comes from

why it is so noisy

what action you took

and explain why you mention this.

思路延展

第一语组：明确具体的"噪声及来源"，讲述噪声产生的时间、地点、持续时长等信息；

第二语组：回应"噪声巨大的原因"，可能会涉及与施工设备等相关的专业词汇；

第三语组：具体回应"采取的行动"，同时介绍各种措施的有效性；

第四语组：重点回应"自己的举动所产生的意义"。

高分范例

The huge continuous noise from the construction site near our community compound made me very furious. It was 200 metres west of our compound and they were building another condominium. However, can you imagine that they even worked and built at night, after 10 o'clock? They worked day and night, Monday through Sunday, and even in the period prior to the college entrance examination. People living nearby had trouble falling asleep due to the noise from the roaring engines, hammers hitting nails and shouting between workers, and many of us soon became sleep deprived. The construction team worked with such high intensity, though it was a violation of the laws, to shorten their working period, which would be extremely profitable. My neighbours and I took actions to stop this noise by calling the government hot-line and the hot-line of TV stations and newspapers. We even paraded in the street to display our slogans. Through our efforts, we reached an agreement that they had to stop working at 9 pm sharp each day. People in our community finally got back to regular life. The reason I mention this is to highlight the importance of regulation enforcement in modern cities, which is the foundation of society in which everyone's rights are protected. On the other hand, when our rights are infringed upon, we should take action to protect our interests.

亮点句型

- They worked day and night, Monday through Sunday, and even in the period prior to the college entrance examination.
- People living nearby had trouble falling asleep due to the noise from the roaring engines, hammers hitting nails and shouting between workers, and many of us soon became sleep deprived.

地道表达

- construction site 建筑工地
- condominium 公寓
- prior to... 在……之前
- sleep deprived 失眠，缺觉
- violation of the laws 违反法律
- extremely profitable 特别有利可图的
- rights are infringed upon 权利被侵犯

8. A paid job

Describe a paid job you did and enjoyed.

You should say:

what the job was

when and where you did it

what you did

and explain why you enjoyed the job.

思路延展

第一语组：首先明确具体的"工作"，可以是全职的工作也可以是兼职的工作；

第二语组：回应"何时何地"等具体的背景信息，描述当时的工作状态；

第三语组：具体回应"工作内容"，可包括系统的训练、具体的实际操作等；

第四语组：重点回应"喜欢这份工作的原因"，如可以让自己更独立、积累经验、培养能力、塑造性格等。

高分范例

The very first paid job I ever had was the part-time job I took when I was a high school student. I have to say that I did enjoy it though it was extremely laborious, and each time I finished the job, I was completely exhausted. Even though I did not have to support myself by working part-time during college, I thought it would be fun so I applied for a position at KFC as part-time staff during the summer holidays, working four hours each shift. The KFC was not far, about two stops west from where I lived. Prior to working at the kitchen, I first received systematic training about the basics such as how to get the chicken prepared and cooked as well as how to make burgers and French fries. Ironically, the work I spent the most time doing was actually making salad, which was not covered in the training at all. I particularly enjoyed that working experience not for the salary, nor for the free chicken I got each week, but for the friends I made there and the fun I had while working. More importantly, I realised how hard it was to work and to earn myself a living, and I also realised the importance of staying competitive in our increasingly challenging job market. So those great days gave me a lot of good memories and helped me to become more mature.

亮点句型

- The very first paid job I ever had was the part-time job I took when I was a high school student.
- I have to say that I did enjoy it though it was extremely laborious, and each time I finished the job, I was completely exhausted.
- I particularly enjoyed that working experience not for the salary, nor for the free chicken I got each week, but for the friends I made there and the fun I had while working.

地道表达

- very first 第一个
- apply for... 申请······
- shift 轮班
- systematic training 系统化的培训
- earn oneself a living 养活自己

9. A piece of good news

Describe a piece of good news you received.

You should say:

    what the news was about

when you got this news

where you got this news

and explain why you think it was a piece of good news.

思路延展

第一语组：明确具体的"消息"，说明消息的内容；

第二语组：回应"获得该消息的时间"，阐述事件背景；

第三语组：回应"获得该消息的地点"，可以具体到消息的获得方式、通知这条消息的人等；

第四语组：重点回应"对自己来说是好消息的具体方面"，如为自己带来好的影响、使自己心情愉悦等。

高分范例

The news that thrilled me was the one I got last month. My professor told me through an email that the 300-page academic paper that I had submitted impressed the judges of the school committee. When I got the news, I was having dinner with my parents in a fancy restaurant on a Sunday last month. I couldn't help but shout out in excitement. For me, it was the best news ever. My years of continuous research and hard work had finally paid off. During the past several years, I had to collect and analyse data, being critical of what I read and what my teammates shared. Sometimes, I even had to rewrite the part rejected by the professor. But besides the reward to my efforts, the honour I won and the opportunity to show off, it also gave me the encouragement to continue exploring this field based on the groundwork laid by this paper. In the future, many academic forums and seminars may also open their doors to me since I have participated in some leading research projects and worked with teammates from top universities under the guidance of renowned professors.

亮点句型

- The news that thrilled me was the one I got last month.
- In the future, many academic forums and seminars may also open their doors to me since I have participated in some leading research projects and worked with teammates from top universities under the guidance of renowned professors.

地道表达

- thrill 使……激动
- school committee 校委会
- pay off 成功，奏效
- collect and analyse data 收集、分析数据
- rewrite 重写

- be rejected by... 被……拒绝
- based on the groundwork lay by... 基于……打下的基础
- academic forum and seminar 学术论坛及研讨会

10. A positive change

Describe a positive change you have made.

You should say:

what the change is

when you started this change

why you made this change

and explain how this positive change benefited you.

思路延展

第一语组：明确具体的"积极变化"，可以是性格、思维方式、个人状况等方面的变化；

第二语组：回应"开始改变的契机"，叙述时间、地点等相关背景信息；

第三语组：具体回应"做出改变的原因"，结合上述信息进行解释与说明；

第四语组：重点回应"这一积极的改变带来的益处"，可从 2 ～ 3 方面进行阐述。

高分范例

The most important positive change in my life would be the way I have changed my perception of the world, which has transformed from merely accepting without question to thinking critically and independently, which happened in my college life. This was closely related to my working experience as chairman of the students' union. At first, my personality adversely affected my work efficiency because I took others' opinions too seriously and could never finalise the plan. Sometimes I would lose my stance amid group discussion, especially when there was an opposite voice from another union member. My teachers and classmates began questioning my working ability, and that was when I decided to make a change. I reflected on myself and tried to find out where the problem lay. Then I realised that I was afraid of taking responsibility, which is a characteristic that a leader should not have. So each time, I tried to consider all the factors thoroughly and whenever I made up my mind after careful evaluation, I stuck to my guns and tried to persuade people on the other side, so that I could settle the issues more quickly. With the help of such changes, I have become a decisive leader and set a clear direction for the future progression of the union.

亮点句型

- The most important positive change in my life would be the way I have changed my perception of the world, which has transformed from merely accepting without question to thinking critically and independently, which happened in my college life.
- My teachers and classmates began questioning my working ability, and that was when I decided to make a change.

地道表达

- accept without question 不加质疑地接受
- make a change 做出改变
- reflect on oneself 反省
- stick to one's guns 坚持自己的意见

11. A recent law

Describe a recent law about environmental protection.

You should say:

what it is

when it took effect

why this law is established

and explain how you feel about this law.

思路延展

第一语组：首先明确具体的"法规"；

第二语组：回应"生效时间"，介绍背景；

第三语组：具体回应"建立此法规的原因"，例如环境问题、环境保护的紧迫性等；

第四语组：重点回应"自己的感受"，可涉及法规实施情况、带来的效果，人们对法规的评价等。

高分范例

When it comes to a law about protecting the environment, I'd like to talk about the one that prohibits the use of plastic bags without charge. Previously, it was common for us to ask for two or three plastic bags for free when shopping at supermarkets. However, a few years ago, this behaviour was put to a stop as our government launched a policy that required customers to pay for plastic bags used for packing goods, and they were encouraged to take their own shopping bags or baskets. This policy has been in effect for several years, and more and more people have cultivated the habit of bringing their own bags when shopping.

I think this law was really a necessity, since the environmental pollution was rather serious then. Without proper treatment, some plastic bags even flew into the ocean, and some aquatic animals may mistake plastic bags as jellyfish, which causes suffocation when animals swallow them. Besides, plastic bags are almost non-biodegradable, staying intact even when buried for decades, which will pollute the earth and underground water. So I believe charging for the use of plastic bags will do much good for our society. People first brought their own shopping bags simply to save money, but now that they have gotten used to it, the use and production of plastic bags will gradually decrease. Through the joint efforts of the government and citizens together, we can better protect the environment.

亮点句型

- When it comes to a law about protecting the environment, I'd like to talk about the one that prohibits the use of plastic bags without charge.

地道表达

- prohibit the use of...　禁止……的使用
- without charge　免费
- launch a policy　推出一项政策
- shopping bag　购物袋
- cultivate the habit of...　养成……的习惯
- suffocation　窒息
- non-biodegradable　不可生物降解的

12. A TV documentary

Describe a TV documentary you watched that was particularly interesting.

You should say:

　　what the documentary was about

　　why you decided to watch it

　　what you learned during the documentary

and explain why the TV documentary was particularly interesting.

思路延展

第一语组：首先明确具体的"纪录片"；

第二语组：回应"观看的原因"，比如有趣的访谈、有意思的实验及意想不到的实验结果；

第三语组：回应"观看的收获"，比如学到的知识；

第四语组：重点回应"对自己来说比较有意思的方面"，如从中学到的方法等。

高分范例

The documentary that captured my attention was called *Fighting Obesity*. It primarily focused on why people gain so much body fat and how people lose weight. I decided to watch this documentary because the host of it was extremely humorous, making the audience laugh. He interviewed different people in each episode, with some experiments. The reason why I did not miss a single episode was that it always provided some unexpected experimental results, which were really eye-opening. I learned a lot of knowledge about how to keep fit through a detailed diet plan and regular exercise. To my surprise, the documentary revealed a research finding that a lot of calories are burned even after we stop exercising, so the number we read in the machine is actually far below the total amount we consume. This encouraged me to exercise more since exercising is far more effective than I previously thought. What made the documentary interesting was the unusual experiments in each episode. The subjects they chose for each experiment were kind of strange, such as the diet of truck drivers or the stomach of soldiers, but they always managed to find something meaningful from all these seemingly irrelevant experiments. For example, they showed people how nutrition could be transformed into muscles rather than body fats after exercising. It reshaped my understanding of obesity and its connection to our living habits, diets and exercise frequency. I learned how to keep fit with the valuable suggestions provided in the documentary while also watching it for relaxation.

亮点句型

- The documentary that captured my attention was called...
- The reason why I did not miss a single episode was that it always provided some unexpected experimental results, which were really eye-opening.
- I learned a lot of knowledge about how to keep fit through a detailed diet plan and regular exercise.
- For example, they showed people how nutrition could be transformed into muscles rather than body fats after exercising.
- It reshaped my understanding of obesity and its connection to our living habits, diets and exercise frequency.

地道表达

- documentary 纪录片
- capture one's attention 引起某人的关注
- obesity 肥胖
- gain body fat 增重
- episode 一集
- experimental result 实验结果
- eye-opening 开眼界的
- be transformed into... 被转换成……
- reshape 改变

13. A useful app

Describe a useful app.
You should say:
    what it is
    when you use it
    what you use it for
and explain why you think it is useful.

思路延展

第一语组：明确要讨论的"应用"，描述具体信息如开发者、主要用途等；

第二语组：回应"什么时间使用"，可以讲开始使用的时间和频次等；

第三语组：回应"使用的目的"，可包含功能描述及特点介绍等；

第四语组：重点回应"该应用有帮助"的具体表现，结合功能特点描述通过这个应用得到的收获。

高分范例

I count on the DP app, a mobile application that features recommendations about where to eat, drink and relax, and more importantly, some strategies to save money. It consists of many functions like the ranks of restaurants based on the ratings from diners, or the popularity of different shopping centres with comments from the consumers. I have been using it from the moment the app was launched, and it offers me valuable suggestions on restaurants to visit. All my friends are also great fans of this app, using it as a guide for the best deal. Each time I plan to eat out with friends, I browse the recommendations first, comparing the pricing and rating of the restaurants. In order to attract more customers, various restaurant owners and investors of the app are usually pretty generous, giving 20%–45% discounts on average. Whenever I browse the app, there are always some promotions. Can you imagine that such an app sometimes even gives out lucky money? The money can be automatically deposited into our e-wallets, tempting us to buy more coupons on the app. This app is extremely helpful as it provides good info with some occasional pleasant surprises. We feel a sense of achievement when the comments and recommendations that we have left on the app are marked as helpful by other customers.

- I count on...app, a mobile application that features recommendations about where to eat, drink and relax, and more importantly, some strategies to save money.
- I have been using it from the moment the app was launched, and it offers me valuable suggestions on restaurants to visit.
- The money can be automatically deposited into our e-wallets, tempting us to buy more coupons on the app.

地道表达

- mobile application 手机应用
- the ratings from... ……给出的评分
- launch （首次）上市，发行
- the best deal 最佳交易

- eat out with friends 和朋友们出去吃饭
- lucky money 红包
- occasional pleasant surprises 偶尔的惊喜

14. A website you use frequently

Describe a website that you often use.

You should say:

which website it is

what service the website offers

how often you use this website

and explain how this website helps you.

思路延展

第一语组：明确具体的"网站"，描述相关功能特点；

第二语组：回应"提供的服务"，可具体描述该网站各板块的信息、服务与功能等；

第三语组：具体回应"使用的频次"，解释为什么这样高频次地使用该网站；

第四语组：重点回应"如何能够帮到你"，讲出作为用户的受益之处。

高分范例

Well, the website that I frequently visit is HJ English Learning Online, which holds all the resources I need to learn English. It offers a variety of learning material ranging from free courses, to English novels, to articles on learning methods. I can find experienced teachers online as long as I simply enter some requirements in the search engine. The website acts as my suggestion giver, a good guide and a helper. I choose this website out of so many websites I use because it is very helpful for students who are eager to improve their English. The website also offers a bunch of different video resources such as live English news, which help me practise my listening skills. In particular, I can listen to the news at different speeds, slow, fast or normal. I keep visiting the website each day, as the news is updated every day. I use a specially designed method to improve my listening comprehension and expand my vocabulary using this website. Firstly, I type down what I have heard sentence by sentence. Then I click the button of submission, and the website automatically checks my transcripts and highlights the discrepancies, so that I can learn from my mistakes. Thanks to this website, my English has improved immensely over the past three years.

亮点句型

- The website that I frequently visit is..., which holds all the resources I need to learn English.
- It offers a variety of learning material ranging from...to...
- I choose this website out of so many websites I use because...
- Thanks to this website, my English has improved immensely over the past three years.

地道表达

- a variety of... 多种多样的……
- range from...to... 包括（从……到……）之间的各类事物
- search engine 搜索引擎
- suggestion giver 建议的给予者
- a bunch of... 大量……
- live news 实况新闻

15. An article about health

Describe an article about health.

You should say:

when and where you read it

what it is about

what it suggests people do

and explain why you believe it is very helpful.

思路延展

第一语组：明确具体的"文章"，说明文章主题，如健康饮食等；

第二语组：回应"主题下具体的内容"，如饮食的分类、建议等；

第三语组：具体回应"建议人们做的事情"；

第四语组：重点回应"比较有帮助的方面"，具体说明是如何受益的。

高分范例

I just read an article in the newspaper about the best diet in summer a few days ago, which I believe should be extremely informative for people who are tortured by the sweltering weather in Jinan. The article discusses at great length what people should eat in summer, which is the same thing that has been repeated in other health-themed articles. But the following part about what people should avoid eating is really eye-opening. The logical explanations accompanied with annotated pictures explains in detail how cold food helps illnesses sneak up on people and how health problems in autumn and winter stem from summer. It also points out how cold food interferes with the secretion of hormones in the endocrine system, even though people feel cooler while having iced beverages on hot summer days. Then comes the part about spicy food, which I should say has totally reshaped my dietary habits. The article points out that some people's digestion systems are not used to the stimulation caused by spicy food, and regular intake of spicy food for this group of people could possibly lead to serious illness. So I quit my unhealthy diet and now try to eat things with milder flavours. With months of healthy eating, my body has become quite fit and I feel rejuvenated. I owe my healthy physical condition today to the guidance of this article. It also reminds me that it is really important to maintain a healthy lifestyle.

亮点句型

- But the following part about what people should avoid eating is really eye-opening.
- Then comes the part about the spicy food, which I should say had totally reshaped my dietary habits.

地道表达

- informative　提供有用信息的
- be tortured by...　被……折磨……
- sweltering　酷热难耐的
- accompany with...　带有……
- annotate　注释
- sneak up on...　偷偷走近……
- stem form　源于

- interfere with...　干扰……
- secretion　分泌
- hormone　激素
- endocrine system　内分泌系统
- dietary habit　饮食习惯
- regular intake　规律的摄入

16. An article you read

Describe an article you read in a newspaper or magazine.

You should say:

    when and where you read it

    what it was about

    why it attracted you

and explain what you would do after reading it.

思路延展

第一语组：首先明确具体的"文章"，并介绍阅读的具体时间与地点；

第二语组：回应"文章的主题"，延展题材、内容及配图等细节信息；

第三语组：回应"文章内容吸引你的原因"；

第四语组：重点回应"读后的行动"，包括具体的计划与想法、行动与体验等。

高分范例

The article I would like to talk about was about a top university named UBC in Canada. When I was sitting in a café waiting for my friends, I grabbed a magazine randomly, and one of the article's titles captured my attention. The article spent its first section talking about the facilities and teaching resources at UBC, which almost put me off from reading further. But I was soon drawn in by the paragraphs about campus activities and academic life, accompanied by vivid photos of students holding club events. The article painted a lively and diverse picture of university life in my mind and I really admired the level of freedom and autonomy the students seemed to have over their curriculum and timetable. I was inspired to study in such a university so that I could explore different fields. So, I made my own plans. I planned to take some summer courses in UBC on campus to have the real personal experience of studying at UBC first, and interacting with the students and faculty there. I also left my contact information at the student office, so that I could receive further notices whenever some courses are updated. I would be happy to have a guided tour on the campus.

亮点句型

- The article I would like to talk about was about...
- The article spent its first section talking about..., which almost put me off from reading further.
- But I was soon drawn in by the paragraphs about...

- grab a magazine　抓起一本杂志
- randomly　随意地
- put sb. off from reading further　让某人对继续阅读失去了兴趣
- autonomy　自主权
- curriculum　课程
- guided tour　有导游的游览

17. An important experience

Describe an important experience of learning a skill.

You should say:

what the skill was

who you learnt it from

how you learnt it

and explain why you think the experience is important.

思路延展

第一语组：首先明确"学习的技能"是什么，进行主题回应；

第二语组：回应"教你这项技能的人"，介绍此人的背景、专业等；

第三语组：具体回应"学习的方式"，分别介绍各个步骤、练习方法等；

第四语组：重点回应"为什么觉得这次经历重要"，可描述收获和意义等。

高分范例

Of the many things I have mastered successfully, the experience of learning how to swim would be the story I want to share at this moment. It went like this: I was frequently laughed at by my friends because I was kind of clumsy and could never swim without a swimming ring. One day, I decided to give it a try. I took several steps to try to break through this barrier. The first thing I did was to learn some theories about swimming through reading books and watching some training videos online. Then, I took a training course in a gym, where a professional instructor patiently taught me the movements and some tips in detail. In a few days' time, I quickly mastered the movements of my arms and legs, the timing of breathing in and out, as well as some precautions when swimming. After practising for a couple of days, I became a strong swimmer. The whole experience encouraged me to step out of my comfort zone. You never know what you can achieve until you try, so just keep trying. Plus, the systematic approach to learning swimming helped me make rapid progress, which built up my confidence. Even if I am faced with difficulties in learning other things, I believe that all I need to do is keep trying.

亮点句型

- Of the many things I have mastered successfully, the experience of learning how to swim would be the story I want to share at this moment.
- The first thing I did was to learn some theories about swimming through reading books and watching some training videos online.
- Then, I took a training course in a gym, where a professional instructor patiently taught me the movements and some tips in detail.

地道表达

- break through　突破
- breath in and out　吸气与呼气
- some precautions　一些注意事项
- a couple of days　几天
- step out of one's comfort zone　走出某人的舒适区

18. An important festival

Describe an important festival.

You should say:

　　what it is and when

　　what special meaning it has

　　what people usually do during this festival

and explain why it is important / why you like it.

思路延展

第一语组：首先明确具体的"节日"，说明该节日的日期及相关信息；

第二语组：回应"该节日的特殊意义"；

第三语组：具体回应"人们在该节日会做的事情"，介绍相关的庆祝活动、游戏等；

第四语组：核心内容，重点回应"该节日的重要性"或"喜欢该节日的原因"。

高分范例

Apart from the big festivals like the Spring Festival and the Mid-Autumn Festival, the one I value the most is the Lantern Festival. It is on the fifteenth of January on the lunar calendar and it means the end of the Spring Festival. The traditional activities include eating Yuanxiao and viewing lantern shows. People generally eat Yuanxiao at dinner, and go out to appreciate the lantern shows in the streets and parks afterwards. The most important part for lantern shows is guessing lantern riddles. The traditional lanterns always have riddles with various topics. These activities are not actually confined to the lantern shows only; people may hold this riddle-guessing activity at home throughout the whole Spring Festival. From my childhood, I always tried my best to guess the answers of the riddles so that I could beat my cousins in the competition, and I could often get a lot of lucky money from my parents when I came up with correct answers. This festival is extremely meaningful, especially the riddle-guessing part, because it broadens people's understanding of rich traditional Chinese culture.

亮点句型

- Apart from the big festivals like the Spring Festival and Mid-Autumn Festival, the one I value the most is the Lantern Festival.

地道表达

- apart from 除了
- lunar calendar 农历
- traditional activity 民俗活动
- be confined to... 被限于……

- broaden the understanding of... 增加对……的了解
- traditional chinese culture 中国传统文化

19. Favourite season

Describe your favourite season.

You should say:

　　what season it is

　　what the weather is like at that time

　　what you usually do at that time

and explain why you enjoy that season.

思路延展

第一语组：首先明确具体的"季节"；

第二语组：回应"该季节的天气特点"；

第三语组：回应"在该季节会做的事情"，如户外运动等；

第四语组：重点回应"喜欢该季节的具体原因"，如宜人的气候、美味的水果、收获的感受等。

高分范例

If I am to speak of my favourite season, I would choose autumn without any hesitation. I am kind of fascinated by the weather in this season because it results in beautiful scenery thanks to the gold and scarlet leaves that decorate the trees, as well as the crisp and cool air. During autumn, the temperature ranges from 18 to 28 degrees centigrade. It is neither too hot nor too cold for outdoor sports, and the weather is usually sunny and cool for picnicking or hiking with a bunch of friends, which is a must for me in such a season. Another thing I also like to do is morning exercise. I usually jog around my neighbourhood every autumn morning, enjoying the crisp and moist air. During this season, I also enjoy reading in my study, with a cool breeze gently coming through the windows. Autumn is the season of harvest, so while I have a great variety of fruits to eat, I also realise how important it is to cultivate the land in the spring if we want to have an autumn with a rich harvest.

亮点句型

- If I am to speak of my favourite season, I would choose autumn without any hesitation.
- It is neither too hot nor too cold for outdoor sports...

地道表达

- crisp and cool air　清凉的空气
- a great variety of...　各种各样的……
- in addition to...　除……之外

20. Perfect weather

Describe a day when you thought the weather was perfect.

You should say:

　　where you were on this day

　　what the weather was like on this day

　　what you did during the day

and explain why you thought the weather was perfect on this day.

思路延展

第一语组：明确具体的"一天"，描述良好的天气状况，回应主题；

第二语组：回应"这天的天气情况"，可拓展相关的地点、活动等；

第三语组：具体回应"这天做的事情"，可以分别描述白天的活动、晚上的活动等；

第四语组：重点回应"认为这天天气很完美的原因"，可描述活动带来的感受等。

高分范例

I would like to talk about last Saturday, when the weather was extraordinarily good in my city. I was initially at home, and when I was doing yoga on my balcony, I realised that I could clearly see the whole neighbourhood and the hills a few miles away from the 29th floor of my apartment building. The air was clean and fresh after several days of rain. I thought it would be a waste to stay at home for a whole day, so I asked my friends out and we went hiking in the hills. The humid and gentle breeze kissed my skin and adorable squirrels jumped between trees. Walking on the path deep in the forest, I breathed the fresh air deeply, and that was when I managed to reach inner peace. In the evening, when we finally finished hiking, I sat on a bench in the neighbourhood and watched the setting sun painting the cloud in scarlet red. When night finally came, though there was still some light pollution, I was met with a starry night, and tried to recognise as many constellations as I could. I thought the weather was quite excellent on that day, and I really got the chance to immerse in beautiful nature with a light heart.

亮点句型

- I would like to talk about last Saturday, when the weather was extraordinarily good in my city.

地道表达

- the whole neighbourhood　整个社区
- humid and gentle breeze　潮湿和煦的微风

Notes

第五节　地点类 Places

1. A big company

> Describe a big company that you want to visit.
>
> You should say:
>
> what it is called
>
> how you know the company
>
> what business the company does
>
> and explain why you want to visit this company.

思路延展

第一语组：明确具体的"公司"名称，可以列举平时比较熟悉的公司；

第二语组：回应"知道这家公司的途径"，例如通过公司网页、新闻、产品发布会等；

第三语组：具体回应"这家公司的业务类型"，可能涉及一些专业词汇，需要有所准备；

第四语组：重点回应"想去参观的原因"，可描述这家公司的一些理念，以及自己对这些理念的感想等。

高分范例

The company that has never failed to capture my attention and imagination is Huawei. It is a supergiant in the IT industry and it has subsidiaries all over the world. I should say I get the ins and outs about it through browsing its official website and reading relevant news reports. I also search the profiles of its successive CEOs, getting some insights about this company. But most often, I browse pictures of the interior environment of the company, which is a unique way to learn its ambience and corporate culture. Its products include mobile phones, mobile broadband terminals, terminal cloud, etc. With its own global network advantages and global operation capabilities, it is committed to bringing the latest technology to consumers. It constantly upgrades the technologies behind the products, and often brings surprises to customers. I would be extremely happy if one day I could visit its headquarters, and have a guided tour while meeting the technicians, experts and managerial staff there.

亮点句型

- The company that has never failed to capture my attention and imagination is Huawei.
- But most often, I browse pictures of the interior environment of the company, which is

a unique way to learn its ambience and corporate culture.

地道表达

- **never fail to do sth.** 从未失败于做某事
- **supergiant** （某领域的）巨头
- **subsidiary** 子公司
- **ins and outs** 详情
- **interior environment** 内部环境
- **be committed to...** 致力于……
- **headquarters** 总部

2. A busy street

Describe a busy street / a crowded place where you like to go.

You should say:

where the place is

when you go there

what you do there

and explain how you feel about the crowded place.

思路延展

第一语组：明确具体的"地方"，与提纲中的 where 结合介绍该地方的位置、作用等相关信息；

第二语组：回应"什么时候"，介绍自己通常在什么情形下去该地方；

第三语组：回应"做什么"，解释自己去该地方的原因，介绍其特点、拥挤程度等；

第四语组：具体回应"自己的感受"，阐述在这个地方获得的愉悦以及拥挤带来的各种不便等。

高分范例

The crowded place that I will share at this moment is Quancheng Road in Jinan, where numerous stores, supermarkets, diners, vendors and boutiques are located. Complexes like Plaza 66 and high-end shops of great variety are scattered along the road. I often go there on weekends, in the company of a bunch of friends, and I should say that the place is a combination of heaven and hell. We usually do a lot of things there, such as dining, shopping and watching movies. But I have to say that most of the time we are just waiting and changing our plans. Since there are, statistically, up to nearly 200,000 people in this street on a single day at weekends on average, we usually have to spend 50 minutes driving once we enter the underground parking garages to find a parking space. Then comes the nightmare of the long queue in each store or restaurant, so we have to take a number, sit on the chairs outside and complain on social media like WeChat. In order to save time, we often change our plans such as watching movies before dinner to avoid peak hours, but it doesn't help since it's always crowded nearly everywhere. The more I love this place, the more I hate it. Although it caters to all our needs, the masses of people there always ruin a wonderful day. The reason I still choose to go there each time is that we all enjoy the delicious food there.

亮点句型

● Since there are, statistically, up to nearly 200,000 people in this street on a single day at weekends on average, we usually have to spend 50 minutes driving once we enter the underground parking garages to find a parking space.

地道表达

● complexes　建筑群

● high-end　高档的

● of great variety　多样的

● statistically　统计上地

● underground parking garage　地下车库

● parking space　停车位

● avoid peak hours　躲开高峰期

3. A café

Describe a café that you know in your hometown.

You should say:

where it is

how often you go there

what kind of food they serve there

and explain why you choose this place.

思路延展

第一语组：首先明确具体的"咖啡馆"，进行主题回应，细化地点、风格、顾客群等信息；

第二语组：回应具体的"频次"，并解释此频次出现的原因；

第三语组：具体回应"食物的类别"，可进一步介绍其主营餐品及其特点等；

第四语组：核心内容，重点回应"选择这里的原因"，如氛围、品质等。

高分范例

Well, the café I would like to talk about is one that I am quite familiar with. It is located in the community in which one of my friends lives and it is actually owned by her family. It is a western style café. Differing from most of the cafés in town, it mainly caters to foreigners and those who particularly enjoy an exotic style. I go there on Sundays, nearly every week, to have a sip of the coffee my friend specially made for me and read some books there. It serves western food and most food ingredients are imported from Europe, and foreign friends enjoy these very much because of their authentic taste, which reminds them of their home countries. The café is under a hundred square metres in size, so it's small but cozy. The European elements and distinctive flavours have attracted people all over town, so the café is always packed with people. You will have to reserve in advance. I like the feeling of sitting there with a cup of coffee, during a peaceful afternoon in particular. I also enjoy the music played there and the relaxed ambience at the café, which helps me enjoy my moments of solitude.

亮点句型

- It is located in the community in which one of my friends lives and it is actually owned by her family.
- The café is under a hundred square metres in size, so it's small but cosy.

地道表达

- differ from... 与……不同
- cater to... 满足……的需要
- exotic style 异国风格
- have a sip of... 喝一小口……
- under a hundred square metres in size 大小不足一百平方米
- moments of solitude 独处的时光

4. A metropolis

Describe a metropolis.

You should say:

where it is

what you can see in the city

how big it is

and explain how you feel about the city.

思路延展

第一语组：首先明确具体的“城市”并进行简单介绍；

第二语组：回应“在这个城市可以看到的事物”，如建筑及其风格、人们的生活等；

第三语组：回应“城市的规模”，可通过对比来体现；

第四语组：重点回应“自己的感受”，可从 2 ～ 3 方面论述自己对该城市的印象。

高分范例

The metropolis that has impressed me the most is Shanghai. It is a provincial administrative region and municipality directly under the Central Government of China. Shanghai is located in the east of China, adjacent to the East China Sea in the east and Jiangsu and Zhejiang Provinces in the north and west. The first things people will see when they come to the city would be the construction, skyscrapers, and then the highly developed public transportation. The city is big, many times as big as our medium-sized ones. I think Shanghai is a great city. It combines modern buildings, high technology and historical districts preserved, mirroring the history it has experienced. It brings together almost all good worldwide resources, like Fortune 500 companies, headquarters of international corporations, as well as branches of the best overseas universities. It is also the city where people from different backgrounds interact and where ideas from different cultures meet and merge. It is full of energy, hope and vitality, and I believe it is a super place to study, work and live.

亮点句型

- Shanghai is located in the east of China, adjacent to the East China Sea in the east and Jiangsu and Zhejiang Provinces in the north and west.
- It brings together almost all good worldwide resources, like Fortune 500 companies, headquarters of international corporations, as well as branches of the best overseas universities.

地道表达

- provincial administrative region 省级行政区
- municipality directly under the Central Government 中央直辖市
- adjacent to... 邻近……
- high technology 高科技
- mirror 反映出

5. A polluted place

Describe a seriously polluted place.

You should say:

where it is

what it was like before being polluted

how it is polluted

and explain how you feel about the pollution.

思路延展

第一语组：首先明确“被污染的地点”，描述此地点的功能、特点等；

第二语组：回应“被污染之前的情形”，可与被污染之后的情况进行对比；

第三语组：回应“被污染的原因”，可分层论述，如社会原因、经济原因等；

第四语组：重点回应"自己的感受"，可陈述自己的想法、建议采取的措施等。

高分范例

Well, the place I would like to talk about, which is seriously polluted now, is the ring river near my home. It was deep and clean, and used to be heaven for my pals and me when we were children. People would walk along the river, picnic on the riverbank or just enjoy the pleasant breeze there. To me, it was the place that I could go boating and fishing, which were my favourite childhood activities. However, the regulation on sewage disposal has not been strictly enforced. Factories and industries let their wastewater drain into the river and the river has been seriously polluted ever since. The fish are all dead and the smell of the river is unbearable, making people gag. I am indignant about this, because the owners of factories only focus on making money and neglect the irreversible damage they have caused to the environment. Birds, fish, dragonflies and other creatures all died out in this area. For the residents, they have also lost a good leisure place. I believe shared effort is needed to clean the river. The government should step in and set a clear standard for sewage treatment and residents can voluntarily clean up the rubbish floating on the river.

亮点句型

- I am indignant about this, because the owners of factories only focus on making money and neglect the irreversible damage they have caused to the environment.
- The government should step in and set a clear standard for sewage treatment and residents can voluntarily clean up the rubbish floating on the river.

地道表达

- pal 伙伴
- sewage disposal 污水处理
- drain into the river 流入河中
- unbearable 无法忍受的

- indignant 愤慨的
- irreversible damage 不可逆的破坏
- shared effort 共同的努力
- step in... 介入……

6. A public place

Describe a public place that you think needs improvement.

You should say:

    where this public place is

    what it is like

    why you think it needs improvement

and explain how to make it better.

思路延展

第一语组：明确具体的"公共场所"，介绍其名称、位置、历史等；

第二语组：描述其"目前的状况"；

第三语组：论述其"需要改善的方面"；

第四语组：论述"相应的改善措施"，可延伸讨论改善的意义。

高分范例

The place that I think should be temporarily closed for renovation is the City Theatre, which is located downtown. It looks like a building from the 1970s because of its old facilities. I believe it should be improved since the colour of the interior is kind of dull and the walls should be repainted in green and gold to make the ambience livelier. The ticket office should be relocated to a more spacious place so that there could be more room for people to line up. I think the rows of seats should be reduced so that there could be much legroom and the audience could have a much more comfortable time there. Wheelchair accessible routes and seats should be added to offer wheelchair users a barrier-free passage. A central air-conditioning system should be installed so that it would not be hot and stuffy in the summer. The lifts inside the theatre could be upgraded to accommodate more people. Shops that sell books, CDs and souvenirs could be opened to attract more visitors. A larger stage with more sophisticated and advanced lighting and sound systems could be installed with government funds. I think this theatre could become much more popular and even become a major tourist attraction after these improvements.

亮点句型

- The place that I think should be temporarily closed for renovation is the City Theatre, which is located downtown.

- The ticket office should be relocated to a more spacious place so that there could be more room for people to line up.

地道表达

- be temporarily closed　被临时关闭
- kind of dull　有些沉闷
- line up　排队
- legroom　（汽车、飞机、剧院等座位前的）供伸腿的空间，放腿处

- wheelchair user　轮椅使用者
- barrier-free passage　无障碍通道
- hot and stuffy　闷热
- lighting and sound systems　声光系统

7. A quiet place

Describe a quiet place you have found.

You should say:

    where the place is

    what the place looks like

    when you found the place

and explain what you feel about it.

思路延展

第一语组：明确具体的"地方"，介绍其位置、名称等；

第二语组：回应"该地的景观与设施"，可介绍其环境、内部结构等；

第三语组：结合"发现的时间与方式"，进一步说明该地方的特点；

第四语组：重点回应"个人感受"，阐述安静的环境带来的好处。

高分范例

I would like to share about a place that is extremely quiet. It is located at an unknown corner of Qushuiting Street, which is a very noisy and crowded place full of visitors Monday through Sunday. It is a small area where there are a lot of trees, and a small pond with a pavilion on one side. Few people know of the place apart from those who live around it. I found the place last summer when I got lost and came to this unknown corner by chance after I had gone through a complicated network of hutongs. From then on, I often go there with my friends. We can play chess there while drinking tea and making small talk. Sometimes I go there alone, and enjoy the solitude. This quiet place always calms me down. Whenever I am there, I can feel that the weight on my heart lightens and my cloudy mind becomes clearer. So, this is the place I deem my quiet place.

亮点句型

- It is located at an unknown corner of Qushuiting Street, which is a very noisy and crowded place full of visitors Monday through Sunday.

地道表达

- Monday through Sunday 周一至周日
- small talk 闲聊
- pavilion 亭子

第 五 章

Part 3 冲刺技巧

IELTS

SPEAKING

口语考试的第三部分（Part 3）在考生获得较高分数方面的重要程度和决定作用是不容忽视的。雅思口语的评测过程是三个部分综合评分，Part 1 是水平初判断阶段，Part 2 基本确定分数区间，Part 3 则是考官决定区间内分数段是上升还是下降的最后决策阶段。要在 Part 3 打动考官，考生必须让自己的回答言之有物、有理有据、见解独到。

Part 3 题目的形式跟 Part 1 很像，但二者在内容上还是有区别的。Part 1 的话题大多是与个人相关的话题，比如个人的家庭情况、个人爱好、个人感受等。Part 3 的话题从 Part 2 延伸而来，通常需要考生就某个论点发表看法。Part 3 的答题时间长度应比 Part 1 的略长一些，控制在 25 ～ 35 秒为宜。但是，关键的评测点还是语言的质量、信息的有效度和密度，以及话题思想的深度。

在回答 Part 3 的题目时，考生会发现这部分的题目类型是多变的。考生在备考 Part 3 时，一方面要对题目类型进行有效的分类，另一方面要根据这些题目的提问类型进行句型、话题、词汇的准备和积累。

Part 3 的题目可分为以下几类：

1. 对比类

- What are the advantages and disadvantages of travelling by plane?
- Do people wear formal clothes more often than before?
- Do you think young people feel the same about shopping at markets as older people?

题目形式：这类题目包含不同形式的对比——过去与现在的对比；现在的观念、做法与将来可能的变化的对比；年轻人与老年人对于不同问题的看法与做法的对比；文化差异的对比；一些事物优缺点的对比等。

考查能力：此类题目考查考生对事物进行评价与比较的能力及逻辑思维能力。考生需要对现象、差异和优缺点等进行不同维度的对比以呈现比较立体的答案。语法方面可能会涉及比较级、最高级、强调句等。在答题策略上可以采用正反对比论证的方法。

2. 方法建议类

- What measures should government and individuals take to keep public places clean?
- Do you think there should be laws to protect the welfare of pets and farm animals?
- Do you think the government should well plan the city?

题目形式：要求考生针对某个问题提供解决方案。所涉及的问题可分为宏观问题，即需要政府、社会等集体力量解决的大问题，如环境、交通、养老、犯罪、经济、建设、科技、医疗等方面的问题；微观问题，如校园生活、学习、社交等方面的问题。

考查能力：考查考生对具体问题进行具体分析并且提出有效建议的能力。对于宏观类的问题，可以分层次分析不同社会力量能够起到的作用，例如政府应出台的政策、法规，社会媒体起到的宣传作用等。对于微观类的问题，可以提出一些相关的个性化建议，例如自己努力解决，查阅资料，寻求同学的帮助、老师的建议和家人的支持等。

3. 原因类

- Why do some children get spoiled at home?
- Why do some people prefer street markets to shopping malls?
- Why do some older people want to be waiters in big cities?

题目形式：要求考生解释某个社会现象、人们的某种想法或行为等的原因。

考查能力：考查考生对原因的分析能力，可以从以下方面进行分层阐述：主观原因、客观原因、历史与传统的原因、社会变化与趋势潮流原因等，也可以就一种原因进行深入分析。相关的表达也要有所储备，比如：primarily because/partially because/simply because/now that/in that/due to/because of/due to the fact that 等。

4. 影响类

- People from different generations live together. Do you think this is a problem?
- What influences do actors and actresses have on young people?
- Does the development of a city influence the area near it?

题目形式：要求考生分析某个事件或某种现象带来的影响，所讨论的话题一般涉及社会现象、经济发展规律、政府决策、科技发展、学校教育以及流行趋势等。

考查能力：考查考生组织信息和逻辑推导的能力。考生在论述某个事件或某种现象带来的影响时，无论是积极的还是消极的影响，都要注意各个信息点之间的逻辑关系。

5. 最高级类

- What types of weather do people in your country dislike most?
- Which age group enjoys watching films the most? Why?

题目形式：除了对比类题目会考到比较级，有些题目会要求考生论述各种"最……"的情况。这类题目话题内容涉及社会生活各方面，问题形式包含"最大""最远""最有意义""最有影响""最喜欢""最难忘"等。

考查能力：此类话题考查考生对最高级的掌握情况，并且需要考生对具体原因进行深度拓展。

6. 细化列举类

- What kinds of jobs require higher concentration at work?
- What sorts of letters or emails are the most difficult to reply to?

题目形式：考生要在多类型中选取某一个类型并具体评论。通常该话题下可以选取的种类非常多，需要考生先明确自己偏好的一类，然后进行深度的分析和论述。

考查能力：这类问题属于由大到小、逐步细化的回应类题目。在答题的过程中考生需要恰当举例，有条理地分析特性，能够正确使用比较级句式，在分析原因、列举好处时熟练使用原因状语从句、宾语从句、表语从句、定语从句等。

7. 重要性评论类

- Is it important to preserve old buildings?
- What communication skills are important?
- Do you think it is important to give expensive gifts?

题目形式：此类题目要求考生论述某种事物、事件、行为、现象等的重要性和意义。

考查能力：考查考生从多角度对关键因素起到的决定、帮助与促进作用进行阐述，需要结合影响、分层次进行评述。考生评述时要注意连贯性和条理性。

Notes

Part 3 机经话题分类实战

IELTS

SPEAKING

第一节　生活类 Life experiences

1. By plane

(1) What are the advantages and disadvantages of travelling by plane?

It is the fastest way to go to another city, country or even another continent. The service on planes is always excellent. The seats are very comfortable and the cabin is designed to offer maximum comfort for the passengers. However, the hours on the plane are dull, since people have to sit in their chairs, confined in limited space. The plane is often late for various reasons and airports are usually far from the city centre. Plus, air tickets are also expensive.

地道表达

- continent　大陆，洲
- cabin　（飞机的）座舱
- be confined in limited space　被限制在有限的空间

(2) Is it good to live near an airport?

It is actually very noisy due to the constant landings and take-offs, especially in the quiet night. People would gradually become sleep-deprived if they lived in this area for too long. The airport also takes up a large area of land, so travelling around the area may not be that convenient. Sometimes people have to make detours in order to reach their destinations around this area.

地道表达

- land　着陆
- take-off　起飞
- make detours　绕行

2. Clothing

(1) Do people wear formal clothes more often than before?

Apart from work places where people have to wear uniforms to look more professional, people tend to wear casual sportswear in their free time. Now there are more kinds of clothes for people to choose from and nowadays, people put more emphasis on comfort rather than being confined in formal suits. Wearing comfortable clothes can make people feel relaxed and stay focused on work, and thus, many companies now encourage their staff to wear anything they like during work for a more enjoyable working experience.

地道表达

- sportswear 运动服，便装
- put more emphasis on... 更加注重……
- stay focused on work 保持对工作的专注

(2) When should people wear formal clothes?

Honestly speaking, it depends. People wear formal clothes to show respect when they are having interviews, meeting clients or negotiating with partners. Students have to wear formal clothes when attending some important ceremonies like their graduation ceremony. To conclude, on any important occasion, people need to wear uniforms and formal clothes.

地道表达

- show respect 表示尊重
- negotiate with partners 与合作伙伴洽谈
- graduation ceremony 毕业典礼
- on any important occasion 在任何重要场合

3. Family

(1) People from different generations live together. Do you think this is a problem?

To many people, it is a serious problem because of the generation gaps. There could be conflicts between different generations in ways of thinking, lifestyles and beliefs. However, it may not be a problem for some people. For example, I live with my parents and my grandparents, who are all open and liberal. They respect my decisions and treat me like a friend rather than a childish teenager. We respect the differences between us and thus we can live in harmony.

地道表达

- generation gap 代沟
- way of thinking 思维方式
- liberal 开明的
- live in harmony 和谐共处

(2) How do you get along with your parents?

On the weekdays, my parents take good care of me since I have to study. At weekends, I help my parents with the housework. We respect and care for each other with love. We treat each other more like close friends, unlike many other families, where parents are the absolute authority in the family. My parents and I have some common interests. They love to play video games with me and I enjoy the time spent with them. We can do something we both love together.

地道表达

- in the weekdays   在工作日
- absolute authority   绝对的权威
- common interests   共同爱好
- play video games   玩电子游戏

4. Furniture

(1) In your country, where do people buy furniture for their homes?

Well, in each city, there are some plazas specialising in furniture selling, ranging from interior furniture like sofas, tables and chairs, to lighting, carpets, curtains or even some decorative accessories or household gadgets. There is also an IKEA in most medium-sized cities in my country.

亮点句型

- there are some plazas specialising in..., ranging from...to...

地道表达

- specialise in...   专注于……
- interior furniture   室内家具
- decorative accessory   装饰性的配饰
- household gadget   居家的小物件

(2) What factors do people need to consider when buying furniture for the home?

Usually there are a couple of things people have to consider, such as the price, the quality, whether it is environmentally friendly, and whether the sizes, the styles and the colours match the design of the house. People will also consider whether the furniture will meet their needs.

地道表达

- match the design of the house   与房子的设计相匹配
- meet one's needs   满足某人的需求

(3) Why do some people like to buy expensive furniture?

Most expensive furniture is well designed and well made, so people never worry about the quality. Besides, brand-name furniture also reflects people's social status and their taste. Finally, some expensive furniture is made of precious materials, which helps to retain the value of the furniture.

地道表达

- well designed　精心设计的
- well made　制作精良的
- reflect people's social status and their
- taste　体现人们的社会地位和他们的品位
- retain the value　保值

(4) What is the difference between furniture in the office and furniture at home?

There are many differences. The furniture at home is usually quite bulky yet comfortable, helping people relax. However, the furniture in the office is usually mono-coloured, dominated by clean and straight lines, giving an air of professionalism.

地道表达

- bulky　庞大的，笨重的
- mono-coloured　单色的

5. Shopping

(1) Why do some people prefer street markets to shopping malls?

Because street markets offer products the shopping malls do not have. People who prefer street markets usually want to buy something cheaper and more economical. Some goods are only offered in street markets like fresh fruits brought directly from the farms. People can bargain with the vendors and even become good friends with them. They soon become regular buyers at the street markets.

地道表达

- street market　集市
- cheaper and more economical　便宜且实惠的
- bargain　讨价还价
- regular buyer　常客

(2) Do you think young people feel the same about shopping at markets as older people?

They feel totally different, I should say. For young people, they are more into high-end brands so they would usually not choose to shop at markets where cheap and low quality goods are sold. However, for older people, they just want something that is durable with prices as low as possible, so they would prefer the markets where they can bargain with the sellers to get more discounts.

地道表达

- totally different 完全不同的
- high-end band 高端品牌
- durable 持久的，耐用的

(3) Why do some people like to buy expensive goods?

Generally speaking, people on high incomes tend to buy expensive goods because they can afford them. Firstly, they could get high quality products that last longer, which means less repair would be needed. Besides, expensive goods can offer extra value. For example, luxury cars, clothes and watches act as a symbol of identity and social status. For certain occupations such as businessmen and executive managers, these expensive products also demonstrate their competitiveness. So it is a smart decision for a certain group of people to buy expensive goods.

地道表达

- people on high incomes 高收入的人
- extra value 额外价值
- symbol of identity and social status 身
- 份与社会地位的象征
- competitiveness 竞争力
- smart decision 聪明的决策

6. Weather

(1) What types of weather do people in your country dislike most?

I should say people dislike haze the most. In winter, people burn coal for the city's central heating system, which causes haze in the city. Haze is similar to fog, but there are tons of harmful particles floating in the air, which cause infection in the respiratory system. People dislike such weather mostly because it is detrimental to our health.

地道表达

- haze 霾
- particle 颗粒，微粒
- float 飘浮
- respiratory system 呼吸系统
- detrimental to health 对健康有害

(2) What jobs can be affected by different weather conditions?

People are all influenced because bad weather firstly affects the public transportation system, which means that delay in train and bus services are unavoidable. People will be late for their work or for appointments. When the weather gets too bad, people will have to stop their work if they do outdoor jobs, like construction work.

地道表达

- public transportation system　公共交通
  系统
- construction work　建筑工程

(3) How important do you think it is for everyone to check what the next day's weather will be?

Well, it is quite essential to learn what the weather will be like in advance. People could prepare for bad weather, such as wearing more clothes, or taking raincoats or umbrellas when necessary. They can avoid driving cars if it is going to rain heavily the next day, because it would be dangerous to drive in pools of water and the rain would decrease visibility. People can reschedule their work and study and reconsider their routes so that the influence of bad weather could be minimised.

地道表达

- decrease visibility　降低能见度
- reschedule　重新安排
- reconsider　重新考虑
- minimise　最小化

Notes

第二节 社会类 Society

1. Actors and actresses

(1) What influences do actors and actresses have on young people?

As the use of social media becomes increasingly popular, celebrities do have greater influence over teenagers in many aspects both positively and negatively. Young people learn from the celebrities and follow them to support charitable causes. For example, fans of Avril Lavigne donate to her foundation to support research on Lyme disease. On the contrary, since the young people tend to mimic a lot of the behaviour and appearance of their idols, they may wear expensive clothes or have strange hairstyles to match what their favourite actors or actresses do.

地道表达

- celebrity　名人
- positively　积极地
- charitable causes　慈善事业
- donate　捐赠
- foundation　基金会
- Lyme disease　莱姆病
- mimic　效仿

(2) Can you name another comedic actor in your country?

I don't think I will get into any argument if I say Jackie Chan is also a comedic actor. Though he is one of the most famous action movie stars, there are always funny plots, punch lines and unexpected twists throughout his works. When watching films by Jackie Chan, I often laugh so hard that my stomach aches. After watching so many comedic films, I would say that the films featuring Jackie Chan have never failed to bring a smile to my face.

亮点句型

- I don't think I will get into any argument if I say...

地道表达

- get into argument　争论，争议
- funny plot　有意思的情节
- punch line　妙语
- twist　（故事或情况的）转折

(3) Should actors and actresses be paid more?

Well, yes, I think it makes sense. Actors work in quite a competitive environment and face enormous pressure, so they deserve to be paid more. More importantly, they are also public figures, serving as role models for their fans. All the actors and actresses have to constantly behave in a socially acceptable manner, and their private lives are subject to public scrutiny. Considering the important roles actors and actresses play in their fans' lives and the compromised private time, actors and actresses should be paid more.

亮点句型

- I think it makes sense.

地道表达

- deserve to   值得，应得
- public figure   公众人物
- role model   行为榜样

- be subject to...   经受……，遭受……
- public scrutiny   公众监督
- compromise   妥协

2. Animals

(1) Do you think animals have feelings and rights?

Yes, definitely. Although animals are not as intelligent as humans, animals, especially mammals, have feelings as rich as humans. They can feel happy, angry, fearful and sad. We can observe these emotions in domestic cats, dogs and birds because we spend a lot of time playing or interacting with them. They have the right to live a healthy and happy life, and for wild animals, they have the right to stay at the habitats they have lived in for generations.

地道表达

- mammal   哺乳动物
- domestic   驯养的

- interact with...   与……互动
- have the right to...   有权利做……

(2) Do you think there should be laws to protect the welfare of pets and farm animals?

Yes, definitely. Implementation of such policies helps avoid the abuse of animals. There are currently lots of grey areas where animal abuse can go unnoticed, and coming up with strict regulations and enforcement is a pressing issue. It will help perfect the legal system, allowing all animals to live a healthy and happy life.

地道表达

- implementation 实施
- legal system 法律系统

(3) Are there any wild animals in China that are not found in any other country?

Well, yes, of course. We have some animals that are exclusively native to this land, and the one that everyone is familiar with is the panda. Other typical ones I could say are the manchurian tiger, the golden monkey and some species that have died out in other countries. None of those are as well-known as pandas though, since pandas have such adorable features and are often linked to China.

地道表达

- exclusively 专有地
- be native to... 原产于
- manchurian tiger 东北虎
- golden monkey 金丝猴
- die out 灭绝

(4) How do people in your country feel about the protection of wild animals?

They believe it is a must and that the protection given is far from enough. The government and the NGOs have put in great efforts to implement policies and law enforcement, but poaching and trafficking of protected species still continues. People believe more nature reserves should be set up to protect the natural habitats of wild animals and more efforts are needed from different industries to protect wild animals.

亮点句型

- They believe it is a must and the protection given is far from enough.

地道表达

- far from enough 远远不够
- NGO (Non-Government Organisation) 非政府组织
- put in great effort 做出极大努力
- implement 实施
- poach 偷猎
- traffic （非法）买卖
- nature reserve 自然保护区

3. City development

(1) Does the development of a city influence the area near it?

Yes, there could be a lot of influences. The advance and the upgrade of the city would definitely help raise the land value of the surrounding areas. With urban sprawl, the nearby areas will sooner or later be included in the city's expansion. This means that rural areas will also be equipped with better infrastructures, such as public transportation systems and well-funded schools. After that, there will be more people moving to the areas near the city.

地道表达

- upgrade 升级
- land value 土地价值
- surrounding area 周围地区
- urban sprawl 城市蔓延
- city expansion 城市扩张
- rural area 乡村地区
- infrastructure 基础设施

(2) Do you think the government should plan the city well?

Yes, I think the government should take on this job and plan for urban development. This is extremely important because urban development involves many problems and is extremely complicated. It is the government's responsibility to build social, cultural, and political contexts for the city, develop efficient road maps, and allocate educational, industrial, residential, and commercial districts reasonably. These determine how competitive the city can be, and more importantly, how much potential the city will have for sustainable development.

地道表达

- social, cultural and political contexts
  社会、文化、政治背景
- allocate 分配
- sustainable development 可持续发展

(3) Is the city in which you live quite different now compared with what it used to be?

Yes, I should say that my city has been transformed. Apart from the expansion of the city horizontally, it is now very much a vertical city with dozens of skyscrapers. A lot of old buildings have been demolished, roads widened, and infrastructures upgraded. Plenty of wonderful city plazas and modern residential communities have been built under the urban renewal plan. Thus, I should say that my city has changed dramatically because the ways people live and work have changed a lot.

地道表达

- vertical city 垂直城市
- demolish 拆除
- city plaza 城市广场
- urban renewal plan 都市更新计划

4. Gardens

(1) Do gardens play the same role for old people and they do for young people?

No, they don't. Though they are places for entertainment for both the old and the young, the specific activities vary for people of different ages. It offers old people a place for morning and evening exercises like Tai Chi. Young people enjoy more sport-related activities, ranging from skateboarding, ballgames, to jogging.

地道表达

- Tai Chi 太极拳
- skateboarding 滑板运动

(2) Do you think it's more important to have public facilities, such as gardens and parks, for young people or for old people?

Public facilities are essential for older adults. Unlike young people who have abundant choices, the daily routines and lifestyles of the old are relatively monotonous. Since they spend a high proportion of their time in public places such as parks and community centres where they can play chess, exercise, or simply chat with others, there should be more public facilities for old people.

地道词汇

- monotonous 单调的
- community centre 社区活动中心
- a high proportion of... 很大一部分……

(3) Do you think gardens have any value for children?

Yes, gardens are the places where children can expose themselves to nature, appreciating the beauty of flowers, trees, and sometimes even wild birds, which stimulate their curiosity for nature. By having direct contact with nature, children may have new discoveries while observing the falling of leaves or watching the marching of ants. Gardens are also heaven for children because it is there they can have a quality time playing games with their pals while occasionally meeting some new friends.

地道表达

- expose to 使接触，使体验
- have a direct contact with nature 与大自然有直接接触
- stimulate one's curiosity 引起好奇

(4) Which is more important, public or private gardens?

Public gardens are more important since they serve a greater population. Though the private ones could be personalised and uniquely themed, which reflects their owners' taste, they are underused compared to public ones. Public gardens are the assets of the local community, which ensures their proper management.

地道表达

- serve a greater population 服务于更多人
- uniquely themed 主题独特的
- be much underused 未充分利用的
- asset 资产
- proper management 妥善管理

5. Historic buildings

(1) How do people in your country feel about protecting historic buildings?

Well, people in my country feel it is an important issue to protect historic buildings. They propose measures to protect and preserve historic buildings, and the government and museums work together to restore them to their original state since they are an invaluable cultural heritage of the nation. Historic buildings have been attracting tourists from all over the world, which has always been an important way to promote our national culture.

地道表达

- protect and preserve 保护和维护
- invaluable cultural heritage 无价的文化遗产

(2) Do you think an interesting local historic place is beneficial?

Yes, definitely. Such a place helps decorate the landscape of the city, which is dominated by concrete and steel. The stories of ancient times that happened in the city certainly give the city a mysterious lure, which attracts enthusiasts who are interested in history and cultural heritage to come and visit. The interesting local historic places could become tourist attractions, which would generate revenue, boost local economy and create job opportunities.

地道表达

- lure 吸引力
- tourist attraction 旅游胜地
- generate revenue 创造收入
- boost local economy 促进当地经济发展
- create job opportunities 创造就业机会

(3) What do you think will happen to historic places or buildings in the future?

Historic places or buildings will be better maintained and preserved by the government and experts in related fields. As people come to realise the significance of these cultural heritage sites, the government will allocate more budget for maintenance and repair work and even work out some renovation plans. More policies could be implemented to best protect the historic places. For example, the average number of tourists each day could be controlled so that those places won't become too crowded.

地道表达

- maintain and preserve 维护和保存
- budget 预算
- allocate 分配

6. Old buildings

(1) How do people feel about old buildings?

The feelings vary, and it depends on the type of building. As to the buildings that don't have any historical value and meaning, people just demolish them to make room for modern skyscrapers. However, some historical buildings that are symbols of our culture and heritage are well preserved, and some of them are converted into museums.

亮点句型

- As to the buildings that don't have any historical values and meanings...

地道表达

- make room for... 给……让出地方
- convert into... 改造为……

(2) Is it important to preserve old buildings?

Yes, it certainly is. Some old buildings are important historical relics that historians, architects and many scholars in various fields can study to gain insights into the life and architectural styles of those past periods. While society evolves forward and some traditions have been lost in time, historic buildings will act as a reminiscence of the past, reminding the next generations of our past and cultural roots.

地道表达

- historical relic 历史文物
- reminiscence 回忆，追忆

(3) What aspect of culture do old buildings reflect?

Old buildings mirror the socioeconomic status which the owners of the buildings belonged to and they are also the reflections of architectural styles of ancient times, which are vastly different from our skyscrapers built with steel and concrete. The building materials and decorations used in the buildings show the industrial development, manufacturing ability as well as people's aesthetic fashions of their respective eras.

地道表达

- socioeconomic status 社会经济地位
- building material 建筑材料
- aesthetic fashion 审美时尚

7. Public holidays

(1) Do you think public holidays are important?

Yes, I do. During public holidays, people tend to go travelling, go shopping, visit places of historic interest and scenic beauty, etc., all of which generates purchase behaviour and offers great commercial opportunities. Public holidays also provide ordinary people with some festival ambience, no matter how they spend such holidays. During the holidays people can refresh themselves, mentally and physically.

地道表达

- generate purchase behaviour 产生消费行为
- commercial opportunity 商业机会
- festival ambience 节日氛围
- refresh 使恢复精力
- mentally and physically 精神上和身体上

(2) Do you think there should be more public holidays in your country?

Yes, I do. This will definitely help more people experience quality vacations as more holidays mean that people would be able to travel at different periods. In this way, more people will be able to avoid the milling crowds while enjoying their relaxing holidays with their loved ones. As the saying goes, "All work and no play makes jack a dull boy." I believe more holidays offered by the government could eventually benefit the nation by improving people's mental health.

地道表达

- quality vacation 高质量的假期
- the milling crowds 涌动的人潮
- loved ones 至亲，至爱
- as the saying goes 俗话说

8. Public places

(1) Do older people or younger people prefer exercising in public places?

The public facilities for exercise would be underused without older adults. They tend to exercise regularly in the parks or squares, jogging, dancing or doing martial arts. Exercising in public places allows them to keep a healthy lifestyle and build interpersonal connections. Some senior citizens also enjoy using public places because such sites are free of charge.

地道表达
- martial arts　武术
- senior citizen　老年人

(2) What measures should government and individuals take to keep public places clean?

Firstly, there should be mandatory regulations from the government. Littering and spitting should be strictly prohibited in public spaces. Mass media and schools should take on the role of educating people. As to the individuals, they should follow the laws and behave themselves. No one should ever litter anything in a public place.

地道表达
- mandatory regulation　强制性规定
- the mass media　大众传媒
- littering and spitting　乱扔垃圾和随地吐痰
- take on the role of...　承担……的角色

(3) How do we keep a balance between public places and private houses?

The perfect balance between public places and private houses can be achieved with the help of big data technology. Public places can be built in commercial districts where younger adults tend to gather. Residential areas could be constructed within the 30-minute life circle around the public spaces, and the land value of such properties will naturally grow. The exact number of private houses, shopping malls, and hospitals can also be calculated by utilising a math model based on the age structure of the urban population.

地道表达
- big data technology　大数据技术
- 30-minute life circle　30 分钟生活圈

9. Waiters

(1) How do you deal with impolite waiters?

Well, actually I don't want to waste my time being angry with such people. The way I treat them is just to ignore them. However, if they go too far, I would write formal letters of complaint to their managers, or talk to their managers face to face. This will draw the attention of the management team, urging them to train their waiters with higher standards and improve their service.

亮点句型

- I don't want to waste my time being angry with such people.
- The way I treat them is just to ignore them.

地道表达

- be angry with... 对……生气
- letter of complaint 抱怨信
- management team 管理团队
- urge 促使

(2) Do you think that all waiters should be given training classes?

Yes, I do. I believe untrained staff could cause great trouble, since they may offend customers with impolite tones and behaviour or unprofessional conduct during their service, which would result in piles of complaint letters and the loss of customers. Giving waiters training classes will definitely help improve their service and improve customer satisfaction.

亮点句型

- I believe untrained staff could cause great trouble, since...

地道表达

- untrained staff 未经培训的员工
- offend 冒犯
- unprofessional conduct 违反职业道德的行为
- piles of... 成堆的……
- improve customer satisfaction 提高顾客满意度

(3) Would you like to work in the service industry in the future?

Well, to be honest, I dislike service-sector jobs, because the staff in such fields do not have normal shifts, which means they need to work during evenings or even weekends and holidays. This will trouble me a lot because I won't have time to be with my family when my family members are off. Plus, I want to be an engineer in the future, and thus, I will not consider the service industry.

亮点句型

● This will trouble me a lot because I won't have time to be with my family when my family members are off.

地道表达

- to be honest 说实话
- service-sector job 服务性行业的工作
- off 下班，休息

(4) Why do some older people want to be waiters in big cities?

Some older people from small cities or rural areas may not be well-educated, so without competitive diplomas they can't find good jobs other than being wait staff in big cities. Working as waiters can help them gain relatively high salaries for their family and improve their standards of living. Having any jobs to keep them active greatly reduces the chance of falling ill with senile dementia also. I believe these are the reasons behind this phenomenon.

地道表达

- well-educated 受过良好教育的
- other than 除了
- fall ill 生病
- senile dementia 老年痴呆

Notes

第三节　社交类 Social life

1. Being late

(1) Why are some people always late?

Well, some people tend to procrastinate and thus they can't finish their tasks on time. They are seldom on time, making excuses about the bad weather, oversleeping, or getting into traffic jams. They don't respect their time as well as others' time by keeping others waiting. It is difficult for such a person to change their mindset or habits, since they always lack the willpower to start a task early.

地道表达

- procrastinate　拖延
- make excuses about...　以……为借口
- keep others waiting　让别人等
- mindset　思维模式

(2) Do you think people these days are as punctual as they were in the past?

Well, actually, I personally believe that people are more punctual than ever. In modern society, people value punctuality more as society is becoming more fast-paced. People are always on the way to conferences, to meeting clients or to medical appointments. With the help of many smart tools and courses online, people gradually get the hang of time management and they could use their smart phones to remind themselves of their schedule, so that they could plan ahead and plan out the best routes.

地道表达

- punctuality　准时
- fast-paced　快节奏的
- medical appointment　看诊
- plan ahead　提前计划
- plan out　精心安排

2. Being polite

(1) In what ways do people show politeness when visiting others?

Firstly, people should inform the host way before they visit and bring gifts as a sign of respect. The host will treat their guests with tea or coffee, and sometimes may prepare a good meal. Both the guests and hosts have to follow a code of etiquette so that they won't be regarded as rude.

地道表达

- a sign of respect　表示尊重
- a code of etiquette　礼仪规范

(2) Should people show politeness to friends?

Yes, they should. People need to respect their friends no matter how close they are. Even when they make fun of each other, they need to be careful not to cross the line and offend their friends. Plus, I believe that people should be polite to everyone they encounter, not only friends.

亮点句型

- People need to respect their friends no matter how close they are.

地道表达

- make fun of each other　互相开玩笑
- encounter　遇见
- cross the line　越界

(3) What are inconsiderate behaviours on public transportation?

The list could go on and on. For example, some people do not queue up when buying tickets or some people try to squeeze onto the train or bus without waiting for the passengers to get off first. A lot of people eat and talk loudly to their friends, which can disturb other passengers who are trying to sleep or focus on their work.

地道表达

- queue up　排队
- squeeze onto...　挤上……
- focus on one's work　专心工作

3. Communication

(1) Is it important to learn a foreign language?

Living in the era of the Internet, it is very useful to learn a foreign language, such as English. Most of the resources saved and shared online are in English, so mastering English would allow us to access technologies, fashion and reading materials. It will also make our lives more convenient when travelling abroad since we would then able to communicate with foreigners with ease.

地道表达

- era of Internet 互联网时代
- with ease 轻松地

(2) Has the way people learn a language changed in the past decades?

It has changed a lot. People now tend to learn languages through software and apps, which is more convenient and cheaper. People now also have more chances to study abroad, taking courses in a native environment. In contrast, people in the past only studied languages from teachers in school, or from books or on the radio.

地道表达

- study abroad 出国留学
- in contrast 与此相反

(3) Do you often disagree with others?

I am an easygoing person, so I respect others' opinions and choices. When my classmates and I hang out together or decide something about where to go or what to eat, I always follow their ideas since I don't mind any of the choices. However, sometimes, when we think differently during an academic discussion, I will speak up, and even debate with others over the question at hand.

地道表达

- easygoing person 随和的人
- academic discussion 学术讨论
- debate with others 与他人争论

4. Dining

(1) People often eat with their co-workers nowadays. Do you think it is beneficial?

The benefits are huge and obvious. Employees could casually talk about their problems and exchange ideas with their team members when dining together, which could greatly increase their work efficiency. Compared to formal discussions or meetings, people tend to come up with brilliant ideas in a more relaxing environment. Even if they only have some chitchat that has nothing to do with their tasks, the pleasant respite could strengthen the bonds within a working team. According to a study at Harvard, people perform much better when having closer relations with their co-workers since the working environment helps relieve their stress.

亮点句型

- Even if they only have some chitchat that has nothing to do with their tasks, the pleasant respite could strengthen the bonds within a working team.

地道表达

- huge and obvious　巨大而明显的
- work efficiency　工作效率
- chitchat　闲聊
- respite　暂停，暂缓

(2) Do you agree or disagree that less people eat with their families than before?

Yes, I agree. Nowadays more and more children have begun to go to boarding schools at a young age, where they have to live and study with classmates Monday through Friday. For most adults, they usually have lunch at their workplace, and may work overtime on weekdays and even on weekends. Some of them have to frequently take business trips to other cities or countries. Thus, people on average have fewer chances to eat with their families.

地道表达

- boarding school　寄宿学校
- work overtime　加班工作

(3) Do people eat out more often now than before?

Yes, they do. For students, they attend more parties and group meals, such as birthday parties and graduation nights, to socialise and integrate with the new college community. For employees, they often try out different cuisines or visit bars together after work, releasing stress after a long day of work. Though families with children tend to cook and have meals together at home, most adults find all the steps, such as preparing food ingredients, cooking different dishes and washing the dishes after meals, are too time-consuming. Some of them opt to eat out from time to time so that they can have quality time trying out different restaurants with their family members. Plus, there is a great diversity of restaurants featuring food from different cultures, which are worth trying out.

地道表达

- integrate with...　融入……
- try out　尝试
- prepare food ingredients　准备食材
- time-consuming　耗时的
- opt to do sth.　选择做某事

(4) Why are there so many restaurants in your country?

I think there are several reasons. Firstly, people in my country are proud of their food culture and value the craftsmanship of cooking that has been passed on from generation to generation. Chinese people also enjoy treating others to dinner, and it is our culture to have group meals, celebrating all the significant events such as birthdays, graduations and promotions. What's more, more and more people nowadays tend to eat out instead of cooking at home due to the fast-paced lifestyle and the pressures of modern life. Thus, the catering market has great potential and high profit margins, making people continuously invest a great deal of capital and manpower into this field.

亮点句型

● What's more, more and more people nowadays tend to eat outside instead of cooking at home due to the fast-paced lifestyle and the pressure of modern life.

地道表达

● from generation to generation 一代代
● treat others to dinner 请别人吃饭
● fast-paced lifestyle 快节奏的生活方式
● catering market 餐饮市场

5. Friendship

(1) Do you still keep in touch with friends from your childhood?

Yes, I keep in contact with them regularly. Unlike those friends I made in school or at the workplace, the friends from my childhood know me well and they are more like family. We have created so many fascinating memories together, so hanging with them always makes me happy. Whenever I feel down, they are the ones that I really rely on and seek comfort from.

地道表达

● keep in touch/contact with... 与……保持联系

(2) Is it important for children to have friends?

Yes, children need company. Children need to learn how to work in a team and socialise with others through playing with their peers. Through games, activities, and role play with friends, they'll get to know how to persuade others, how to take the lead, how to cooperate and even how to compromise while respecting different opinions from others. It would be a pity if a child did not have any friends, which could be detrimental to the development of their personality.

地道表达

● work in a team 团队协作
● socialise with... 与……交往

- peer 同龄人，同辈
- detrimental 有害的

(3) Are teenagers more influenced by their peers or their parents?

I believe that though teenagers spend more time with their peers, the influence exerted by parents from a much earlier age is tremendous. They may unconsciously learn from their parents' behaviours, beliefs and even their lifestyles. The way they view the world is very influenced by their parents' education. The influence exerted by their peers is negligible compared to the influence rooted in their mind from their families. Thus, parenting is more important and influential.

地道表达
- exert 施加
- root in... 植根于……
- tremendous 巨大的

(4) For teenagers, do you think they should have lots of friends or just a few good friends?

I am on the side of the latter idea. Quality friendship offers more meaningful socialising experiences. Rather than having tons of friends, having a friend that would lend a helping hand when we are in need is enough. Just as the saying goes, 'A friend in need is a friend indeed.' Having just a few good friends also means that children could spend more time being with their closest friends, building stronger bonds with each other and having friendships that could even last a lifetime.

亮点句型
- I am on the side of the latter idea.

地道表达
- quality friendship 有品质的友谊
- a friend in need is a friend indeed 患难见真情

6. Gifts

(1) Do you think it is easy to choose what to give to other people?

It depends on the recipients of the gifts. For some family members or close friends, we are confident in finding something they would like, since we are familiar with their tastes and favourite things or even know what they yearn for. To pick a gift for someone we are not familiar with is quite a difficult task. We have to guess their preferences, ask for advice from our common friends or search for the right gifts in tons of different gift shops. Since gifts are usually regarded as expressions of the givers' kindly feelings towards the other person, people never find it that easy to choose the right gift.

地道表达

- recipient　接受者
- be familiar with...　熟悉……
- tastes and favourites　品位与喜好
- yearn for...　渴望……，向往……
- be regarded as...　被认为是……
- kindly feelings　心意

(2) Do you think it is important to give expensive gifts?

No, I don't believe so. For me, the gifts I give are to express my gratitude and best wishes for my friends and family. We should not judge the gifts by their monetary value. After all, it's the thought that counts.

地道表达

- gratitude　感激
- count　重要

7. Making friends

(1) How do people in your country make friends these days?

For young people, they make new friends during social activities, such as school parties, clubs, and even on online forums. For adults, they usually make friends at their workplaces, with their colleagues and co-workers that work in the same fields. For the elderly, they make friends with people who have the same exercising schedules as they do.

地道表达

- social activity　社交活动
- online forum　在线论坛

(2) How do you get along with the people you don't like?

I will make an effort to avoid being around such people, so it would not trouble both of us. However, whenever I have to work or study with people I don't get along with, I will focus on the task at hand, and collaborate with them since the priority is to finish the task smoothly.

地道表达

- make an effort　努力

(3) Why do some friendships come to an end?

There are many factors that could end a friendship. When people meet less often, their friendships will gradually end as they no longer keep in touch. Plus, when people do not have some common interests, they won't have any topics to discuss anymore, and thus, they cannot maintain their friendship anymore. There are also many other factors, such as misunderstandings, loss of contact information and busy working schedules, that could cause a friendship to end.

地道表达

- keep in touch 保持联系
- maintain 维持

Notes

第四节 娱乐类 Entertainment

1. Apps

(1) Do you think people could be cheated on apps?

Well, that happens. There are loan sharks that often create wealth-management apps to attract people who need quick money. There are hundreds of those apps recommended to people, and all of them promise a low interest rate. However, the smiling low interest rate will quickly build up, and debt could grow exponentially. What most people are not aware of is that the apps have already stolen information from people's phone contacts during the loan application process. With the information, debt collectors can pester family members and acquaintances of loan takers with phone calls to pressure them into paying off their debts.

地道表达

- loan shark 放高利贷者
- low interest rate 低利息率
- build up 逐渐增加
- grow exponentially 指数级增长
- pester sb. with phone calls 打电话骚扰某人

(2) Is it convenient to use an app?

Yes, it is. Each app is actually smartly developed based on the needs of people. Developers take into account every need people may have based on big data. Thus, those apps offer great convenience. For example, I am using a music-streaming app and all I need to do is just choose the music I like, set the timer, and then I can easily meditate with a smart play list recommended by the app. Also, with the help of this app on my smart watch, my heart rate will be sent to my phone, and the music-streaming app will automatically stop playing after I fall asleep. I could also use it to record the sound of rain, wind, birds singing, etc., so that I can create a customised play list.

地道表达

- base on the needs of... 基于……的需要
- take into account 考虑
- music-streaming app 音乐流应用程序
- set the timer 设置计时器
- play list 播放列表

(3) What are the drawbacks of using an app?

There is a potential downside. Many short video apps are designed to engage people in virtual communities for hours which can be harmful to people's life and health. Indulging in those apps can even isolate people from their family members and significant others. Being addicted to those toxic apps may also lower our work efficiency and pose a threat to family ties.

地道表达

- downside　缺点，不利方面
- virtual community　虚拟社区
- indulge in...　沉溺于……
- be addicted to...　对……上瘾
- pose a threat to...　对……造成威胁

(4) Is using an app more acceptable for young people than old people?

Yes, of course. If young people are passionate advocates of smart devices, many elderly citizens are just passive recipients of touch-screen devices. Young people tend to be more curious and explore their cellphones and new apps, while old people just use some musts, like the apps for communication, transportation or weather reporting.

地道表达

- passionate advocate　热情的拥护者
- passive recipient　被动接受者

2. Cellphones

(1) Is it popular for children to use cellphones in your country?

Yes, it is. Children as young as six begin to use cellphones to communicate with their classmates or play some games for fun, although they are not allowed to use their cellphones on campus. When they are mature enough, often around 13 years old, they usually have their first cellphone, most frequently a used one. So, I should say cellphones are quite popular among children in my country.

地道表达

- on campus　在校内
- used　用过的，旧的

(2) What are the advantages and disadvantages of using cellphones?

Cellphones bring a lot of benefits to our daily lives. Cellphones help enhance the efficiency of work and study. Cellphones enable people to communicate and contact one another quickly and efficiently. They also offer a quick and accurate way for people to share knowledge and exchange opinions. Cellphones have become a multi-functional tool for people to achieve remote working, entertainment, and education. However, people tend to spend too much time on their phones day and night; when they are always connected with people virtually, they may have fewer chances to have essential face-to-face interactions with their loved ones. Thus, overusing cellphones can bring serious downsides.

地道表达

- multi-functional tool　多功能工具
- remote working　远程办公
- face-to-face interaction　面对面交流

(3) What do teenagers in your country use cellphones for?

Apart from using the cellphone to contact their parents and friends, teenagers primarily use the cellphone as a mini computer and a mobile e-purse. They can use their cellphones as a substitute for laptops. Apps in their cellphones can help them concentrate on their work, improve their English skills, listen to audio books, and take better notes. In their routine life, they could use cellphones to order food deliveries, take photographs and videos, and play various games, etc.

地道表达

- mobile e-purse　移动电子钱包
- routine life　日常生活

(4) How do young people and old people use mobile phones differently?

Kids and teenagers use mobile phones more as a game console. Nowadays, most of the popular games offer a mobile edition, which means teenagers can enjoy online gaming with their friends via their mobile phones. Other young adults who are tech geeks are more fascinated by big data and smart algorithms behind apps. They make good use of the e-coupons in apps for discounts, entertaining themselves with top-rated films to watch. They rely on their phones to help them make daily decisions, such as finding the most delicious restaurant, and navigating them to their destinations. To them, mobile phones are more like a highly intelligent hand computer with powerful functions to enrich their lives. However, for older adults, mobile phones may simply be a tool to make phone calls and send messages.

地道表达

- tech geek　科技极客
- smart algorithm　智能算法
- e-coupon　电子优惠券

(5) What is your attitude towards people using mobile phones in public places?

It is fine if people use mobile phones to read or to text. When they talk over the mobile phones in low voices, it is never ill-mannered since others can't overhear. It is quite acceptable for them to watch some videos, even quite funny ones, as long as their mobile phones are connected to their earphones and they don't make weird noises, such as a sudden wow, or some unexpected crazy laugh.

地道表达

- text 发短信
- ill-mannered 没有礼貌的
- overhear 无意中听到
- as long as 只要

3. Internet

(1) What impact has the Internet had on modern people's life?

Well, the Internet has changed and reshaped the life of people as well as the social economy. People nowadays use the Internet to search for information, to shop for what they need, and to receive professional trainings for work. They also enjoy the convenience of on-line banking service, which has totally changed people's approach to wealth management.

地道表达

- search for information 搜寻信息
- wealth management 个人理财

(2) What are the pros and cons of children using the Internet?

Well, it surely has positives and negatives. People are pleased with the fact that children are becoming smarter and they are having a more international worldview. All these aspects could be partially attributed to their use of the Internet to gain knowledge effectively and solve problems independently. However, some children overuse the Internet as their only source of entertainment, indulging themselves in game playing, movie watching, or online chatting, which can have negative impacts on children's health mentally and physically.

亮点句型

- People are pleased with the fact that...

地道表达

- be partially attributed to... 部分归因于……
- overuse 过度使用
- source of entertainment 娱乐资源

(3) Do you think online education is good?

I think online education is extremely good for people in modern society. It saves an abundance of resources, like the cost of time in traffic and the cost of money for constructing or renting classrooms. Online education offers people great conveniences, as people could take online courses whenever and wherever they want. They could also replay the difficult parts of lectures to have a better understanding.

地道表达
- abundant of... 大量……
- online course 在线课程

(4) Do different age groups use the Internet for entertainment in different ways?

Yes, the differences are huge and obvious. For children, they like to play some simple online games which are beneficial to their intellectual development. For adults, they tend to search for information, play online games, watch videos, visit social networks, etc. As for older citizens, they enjoy watching the news and TV programmes.

地道表达
- online game 网络游戏
- social networks 社交网络

4. Movies

(1) How are people influenced by movies?

The ways in which movies could influence the public are various. Firstly, a sense of beauty could be shaped when people see the fancy appearance of characters in movies, like how they dress themselves, what hairstyles they choose, and even what brands of make-up they use. This will definitely influence the way people live. More importantly, some movies could bring about a social trend, making something popular and reshaping social values. Plus, people could get inspiration when watching certain movies, such as detective stories, documentaries, or science fiction films. Thus, movies are becoming a routine for many people, and audiences are being largely influenced whether they are aware of this or not.

地道表达
- the public 大众
- the sense of beauty 美的感觉
- make-up 化妆品
- social trend 社会潮流
- reshape social values 重塑社会价值观
- science fiction 科幻小说或科幻电影

(2) Do people go to the cinema more often now than in the past?

I could say yes or no. Yes, because now there are more well-produced films that entrance audiences worldwide, like *Star Wars*, *Harry Potter* and *The Avengers*. The fancy posters and attractive trailers successfully persuade millions of fans to go to movie theaters and share their joy with similar-minded people. E-coupons for popular movies and well-developed apps which help people book and pay tickets within minutes remove the last barricade for movie fans. Nowadays, people can more easily watch films in well-facilitated cinemas, with 4D screens, IMAX technology, and even Dolby Digital sound effects.

However, I could also say no, since movie-watching costs time and energy. On weekends, people need to spend hours on route to the cinema and many of them may even find no place to park their cars. When they eventually arrive at the cinema, people still need to wait for the films. In most cases, people are even forced to watch some meaningless advertisements before the movie. As a result, all these factors will add up to two or three hours wasted, which is not acceptable for many busy people. So for certain groups, the answer is yes, and for others, it is no.

亮点句型

- E-coupons for popular movies and well-developed apps which...remove the last barricade for movie fans.

地道表达

- well-produced film　制作精良的电影
- entrance　吸引
- fancy poster　花哨的海报
- trailer　预告片
- well-facilitated　设备齐全的
- Dolby Digital sound effect　杜比数字音效
- add up to...　总计为……

5. Music

(1) Do people like to listen to live music?

Of course. Live music is totally different from recorded music. Live music always offers people a sense of involvement especially when their idol is just in front of them. More importantly, it is exhilarating to experience the atmosphere of pure passion and enthusiasm when attending live music events. Interacting with thousands of audience members who have a shared taste in music is also an amazing experience.

地道表达

- sense of involvement　参与感
- exhilarating　令人激动的
- interact with...　与······互动

(2) Is Music an important subject at school in your country?

I don't think so. I should say music is just a required course in primary and secondary school education. However, our education systems, as well as many parents, do not value it as much as they value subjects like Math or Physics. So, for the majority of students, it is just a course they are required to take, but they will not put much effort into it.

地道表达

- required course　必修课
- primary and secondary school education　中小学教育

(3) What kind of music do young people like?

Well, many young people are real music fans and they love many types of music. Some of them love pop songs because they are easy to enjoy. Rock and roll and some heavy metal music is also popular among teenagers since people need these emotional pieces as a catharsis for their pressure. Furthermore, I know countless teenagers listening to K-pop. The use of repetition and powerful beats in K-pop make it a hit at parties.

地道表达

- rock and roll　摇滚乐
- heavy metal music　重金属音乐
- catharsis　宣泄
- K-pop　韩国流行音乐
- hit　很受欢迎的人或事物

(4) What do you think influences a young person's taste in music?

Well, many factors influence one's music taste. Whether they grow up in a family that values music will make a huge difference. The preference and understanding of parents' about music could influence children to some extent. More importantly, children will have their own preference due to the influence of media, friends, and schools. By watching TV shows, listening to concerts, and taking music classes, children will gradually have their own tastes in music. However, I personally believe that they tend to be influenced more by the peer pressure: they will be more likely to choose the music that their friends like.

地道表达

- to some extent　在某种程度上
- peer pressure　来自同伴的压力

6. Newspapers

(1) What are some methods that newspapers use to attract readers?

There are a lot of tricks, like eye-catching titles, creative caricatures, and even some coupons for local businesses. However, long-lasting competitiveness lies in the courage to voice the truth, the immediate reporting of big events, as well as insightful commentary that people would expect.

地道表达

- trick　花招
- eye-catching title　吸引眼球的标题
- caricature　漫画
- local business　本地企业（商店）
- long-lasting competitiveness　长效的竞争力

(2) What influence do you think newspapers have on society?

By capturing the public's attention, newspapers play an essential role in determining the hot-spot of public opinions. The widely debated topics in newspapers could gradually change or even reshape social policies. On the other hand, newspapers could also distract the focus of the masses with some other eye-catching news.

地道表达

- capture the public's attention　吸引大众注意
- hot-spot　热点
- distract focus of the masses　分散大众注意

Notes

第五节 技能类 Skills

1. Being talkative

(1) What jobs need employees to be talkative?

In fact, there are many jobs demanding people to be talkative. Firstly, salespeople need to talk a lot, because while they are introducing the features and functions of their products, they will also have to answer questions, compare pros and cons, and even make small talk with customers to promote mutual feelings. Besides, hosts and hostesses in TV shows have to be super talkative and quick-witted, since their demanding jobs require them to prepare what they are to talk about in the show and they must be ready to improvise at any moment.

地道表达

- salespeople 销售人员
- promote mutual feelings 增进相互的感情
- quick-witted 机智的
- demanding job 要求高的工作
- improvise 即兴创作

(2) Are most Chinese people talkative?

Well, it depends. Extroverts are really talkative in most social occasions. They can talk about trending topics with various people, their friends, co-workers, neighbours, even strangers. For those people, being talkative is a way to express themselves. However, as to introverts, though they have a lot of things on their minds, they do not talk that much. They tend to listen to others during conversations with other people. Many of those introverts value tranquility and they would rather stay alone than talk to others.

地道表达

- extrovert 性格外向者
- social occasion 社交场合
- trending topic 热门话题
- introvert 内向的人

(3) What communication skills are important?

Communication is a complicated task that requires a wide range of skills. One of the most important skills is empathy, i.e., the capacity to understand or feel what another person is experiencing from his/her point of view. More importantly, being polite and showing respect are also important skills that require learning and practice. People need to learn to be culturally sensitive in their communications and avoid non-verbal signals that are potentially aggressive.

地道表达

- empathy 共鸣，同情
- culturally sensitive 文化敏感的
- non-verbal signal 非语言信号
- aggressive 挑衅的，富有攻击性的

(4) Should children be encouraged to talk more?

Yes, I think they should. Being a good speaker requires children to think and organise their thoughts before speaking. Through such practice, children will become more quick-witted with a logical mind and analytical skills. Plus, talking is an important way for children to communicate with others and express themselves. The more they talk, the more likely they will make more friends.

地道表达

- organise their thoughts before speaking
  在说话前组织他们的语言
- logical mind 逻辑思维
- analytical skill 分析能力

2. Concentration

(1) Why are many people addicted to apps?

Some apps are actually too attractive to refuse, even the adults cannot get enough of them. There is a lot of creative content in apps like TikTok and the creators often update their content every day. The more the user creates a playlist and consumes content, the more they will rely on the app. Apps like TikTok are so addictive because the algorithm they use will recommend content based on a users' preferences. Many young people are also fascinated by social media apps because this is where they interact with their friends and classmates.

亮点句型

- Some apps are actually too attractive to refuse, even the adults cannot get enough of them.
- The more the user creates a playlist and consumes content, the more they will rely on the app.

地道表达

- too attractive to refuse　太有吸引力而无法拒绝
- be fascinated by...　对……很着迷
- social media　社交媒体
- interact with...　与……互动

(2) What kinds of jobs require higher concentration at work?

There are actually many jobs that require concentration. Firstly, being a doctor requires one to have a high level of concentration, because doctors need to carefully diagnose patients' symptoms, prescribe drugs, perform surgery, etc. Also, engineers and accountants have to be highly focused because they will have to calculate very accurately, especially the engineers, who have to consider a lot of factors.

地道表达

- diagnose patients' symptoms　诊断病人的症状
- prescribe drugs　开药
- calculate very accurately　精准计算

(3) What kinds of distractions are bothering you in your life?

There are a lot of distractions, actually. When I am at home, I always feel obligated to spend some time with my pet dog. I get distracted when my cute dog comes to me asking for a cuddle. Also, there are often various messages and news being recommended to me on my cellphone and I have to read them quite often. When I am studying in the dorm at school, my roommates may talk to each other, playing games or even enjoying smelly snacks. As a result, there are all kinds of distractions in my life.

地道表达

- feel obligated to do sth.　觉得有义务做某事
- pet dog　宠物狗
- be distracted　被分散精力
- ask for a cuddle　要求抱抱

(4) Have you ever felt it difficult to concentrate?

Yes, I have. When I study one subject for hours, my efficiency declines because I can't keep concentrating. I feel bored doing the same thing for a long time, and my willpower diminishes. Sometimes, when I face some challenging questions, I need to occasionally take a break because being focused on such difficult tasks is extremely exhausting.

地道表达

- the efficiency declines　效率递减
- challenging question　富有挑战的问题

(5) Is it important for children to learn how to concentrate?

Well, it matters. Usually those who succeed in school are those who can focus for quite a long time. Children who can focus on their tasks can learn new stuff more efficiently and will be more likely to find joy while learning. When they grow up, they are more likely to be outstanding workers in their field if they can concentrate on what they do. So, I would say concentration is even more important than their study abilities.

地道表达

- succeed in school 学业成功
- outstanding worker 表现优异的员工

3. Plans

(1) What kinds of plans are practical?

Well, practical plans should be feasible and achievable. I mean when we make a plan, we should consider a number of factors: who is responsible for carrying out the plan, what equipment or tools are required, what additional recourses and supports are needed, when and where the plan will be carried out, and whether or not there could be some unexpected situations. When we take all the factors into consideration, a good plan should be really practical rather than imaginary.

地道表达

- feasible and achievable 有可行性并且是可实现的
- consider a number of factors 考虑一系列因素
- carry out the plan 执行计划
- recourses and supports 资源和支持
- unexpected situation 预料之外的情况
- take all the factors into consideration 将所有因素都考虑进去

(2) How would you tell your friends when you must change your plans?

Well, the first and most important step is to explain the reasons well. I will explain to my friends why I must change my plans and how I am going to compensate for their inconvenience. I will sincerely apologise for my decision and express my regrets for any trouble this change may have caused them. I hope that such actions will help us build mutual understanding. After I gain their support, I will discuss alternative plans with my friends and listen to their insights and opinions.

地道表达

- the first and most important step 第一步也是最重要的一步
- mutual understanding 相互理解
- alternative plan 备选计划
- insight and opinion 见解和观点

(3) What are the common reasons people need to change plans?

Well, there are always some uncertainties that people could never have thought of, like the sudden change of weather or even an accident. On a broader scope, unexpected international political or economic incidents could also force people to change their future plans. People have to make some minor adjustments, coordinating the arrangement of their work and study accordingly.

地道表达

- the sudden change of weather 突然变化的天气
- political or economic incidents 政治或经济事件
- make some minor adjustments 做出微小的调整
- coordinate 协调
- accordingly 相应地

(4) Do old people often change plans?

Relatively speaking, old people change plans less often than young people. Their mindset and behaviour patterns are quite fixed. Thus, when they make plans they will try to make everything certain. Even when accidents happen, they are prone to making small changes rather than dramatic shifts from their original plans. Thus, the frequency for them to change plans is much lower.

地道表达

- relatively speaking 相比较而言
- mindset and behavior pattern 思想和行为模式
- dramatic shift 巨大的变化

4. Subjects

(1) What subjects should be taught in high schools in the future?

Apart from general academic subjects, I think high school students should learn critical thinking and scientific analysis skills. Classes focusing on these topics will help students prepare for their academic explorations in colleges while equipping them with essential skills for their future careers. Plus, subjects ranging from Psychology, Sociology to Economy should also be added to high school curriculums. With the help of the knowledge from those social science classes, students could be much smarter, and they will observe the environment in which they work and live quite differently.

亮点句型

- Classes focusing on these topics will help students prepare for their academic explorations in colleges while equipping them with essential skills for their future careers.

地道表达

- academic subject　学术科目
- critical thinking　批判思维
- academic exploration　学术探索

- equip with...　备有……
- high school curriculum　高中课程
- social science　社会科学

(2) Do you agree or disagree that science is more important than art?

Though it seems that it is science that advances the society and economy, art is actually equally important. People may feel dull without art, and we can see that in more developed countries, art can help society in many aspects. For example, art can inspire people and spark creativity. Successful designers, engineers and even software programmers often appreciate art pieces and take them as their source of new ideas.

地道表达

- feel dull　感到无聊

- spark creativity　激发创造力

(3) What subject do you think is the most important?

I believe that Philosophy is always the most important subject because it provides both the most basic guidance for people to live and the most guiding advice for people to thrive. Philosophy will offer students invaluable skills to view the world critically. Plus, this subject will enable students to master some methods to analyse what they are learning, thus knowing what is important to them.

地道表达

- guiding　给予指导的，有影响的
- view the world critically　批判地看待世界

(4) What methods can be applied to make math class more interesting?

Well, I believe that one of the most important things is to make the students practise using math to solve problems. Teachers can make learning interactive by creating hands-on lessons that involve students every step of the way. Try using a Jigsaw cooperative learning activity in which each student is responsible for his or her own part of a group activity. Or try a hands-on science experiment. When teachers involve students and make lessons interactive, classes will become more interesting.

地道表达

● hands-on lesson   动手课程
● Jigsaw cooperative learning activity   互补式合作学习活动

5. Technology

(1) Do you think technology always has positive effects?

Of course not, because technology is a double-edged sword. While people are enjoying the convenience that technology brings, they have to bear some drawbacks. Even though technology has doubled work efficiency, people are much busier than ever. For example, they have to reply to work-related emails and phone calls even during holidays since it has become easy to reach every person over the Internet. Modern technology brings many new modes of entertainment, such as video games, television and online clips, where people can lay back and relax all day long. Thus, people lack exercise and the obesity rate is on the rise.

亮点句型

● While people are enjoying the convenience that technology brings, they have to bear some drawbacks.
● Modern technology brings many new entertainment means, such as..., where people could lay back and relax for all day long.

地道表达

● double-edged sword   双刃剑
● drawback   弊端
● reach   与……取得联系
● obesity rate   肥胖率
● on the rise   在增加

(2) Do you like to use new technologies?

Yes, I do. It always gives me a totally different experience when using up-to-date technologies. They make my life more convenient, and more importantly, the concepts behind these new technologies are sometimes fascinating and creative, which always inspires me. New technologies also mean some new chances and challenges, which pushes me to learn something new and fresh. Thanks to such new technologies, I can always complete projects with high efficiency.

亮点句型

- It always gives me a totally different experience when using the up-to-date technologies.
- Thanks to such new technologies, I can always complete projects with high efficiency.

地道表达

- fascinating　迷人的

(3) Does technology deeply affect people's lives?

Yes, technology brings tremendous change into people's lives, making people's lives and work easier. For example, people use VR technology for on-line virtual meetings which cuts down travelling time while improving efficiency. Technology connects different sectors in society, making collaboration between different fields possible. For example, mobile payment technology requires a combined effort from IT companies, banks and all the retail shops, making people's life more convenient. Thus, we could say technology has changed the world.

地道表达

- cut down　减少
- mobile payment　移动支付
- combined effort　共同努力
- retail shop　零售商店

(4) Is there any difference between technology in cities and in small towns?

There are some differences. In metropolises like Beijing and Shanghai, new technologies would be launched first so that these large centres always enjoy them first hand and then the technologies would be promoted to other parts of the country quite quickly. In some rural areas, the technologies used there may be outdated and quite a long time may be needed before new technologies are widely used there.

地道表达

- outdated　过时的

(5) How to teach the older generation to use new technology?

As the proverb says, you can't teach an old dog new tricks. This means people tend to be fixed in old habits formed over decades. Although it is difficult to persuade the older generation to try new technologies, it does not mean that they cannot be taught. To help them to learn, the first thing is to be patient, and then teach them step by step. Starting from skills that need to be used daily, for example, calling others and picking up the phone. After many times demonstrating and practising, the older generation can master these skills.

亮点句型

- As the proverb says, you can't teach an old dog new tricks.

地道表达

- over decades　几十年来
- step by step　一步一步地

Notes

高频句型与常用句法

IELTS

SPEAKING

第一节 高频句型

一、肯定回答

- Of course.　当然。
- No doubt.　毫无疑问。
- Definitely.　肯定。
- Absolutely.　对极了。
- That matters.　那很重要。
- That makes sense.　那是有意义的。
- Yeah, it is more my style.　是的，那更符合我的风格。
- I am just the type.　我是这种类型。
- That is my cup of tea.　那符合我的喜好。
- That is exactly what I want.　那正是我想要的。
- That is exactly something rewarding / fascinating / attractive / interesting.　那是非常有回报的 / 迷人的 / 有吸引力的 / 有意思的。
- That is surely something that never fails to capture my attention.　那总能吸引我的注意力。

二、折中回答

- It depends.　这要依情况而定。
- It is hard to say.　这很难说。
- It is hard to response.　这很难回答。
- That is something changeable.　这是可以改变的。
- It varies in different circumstances.　它会根据情况不同而变化。
- It varies for different people.　它因人而异。

三、否定回答

- No, I don't think so.　不，我并不这样认为。
- No, I don't agree with it.　不，我并不赞同这种说法。
- This is not going to happen.　这种情况不会发生。

- My response would be no.　我的回答是"不"。
- That is really something frustrating.　那确实令人有挫败感。

四、表示频率

- I often / frequently / usually / normally do...　我经常 / 通常……
- I never / rarely / seldom / sometimes do...　我从不 / 很少 / 偶尔 / 有时……
- I always do...throughout my education / childhood.　我在整个上学 / 童年时代总是……
- I go swimming twice a week / month.　我每周 / 每月游泳两次。
- I always indulge myself in...on every weekend.　我总是在周末让自己沉浸于……
- I do... just on some special occasions.　我只在一些特殊情况下会做……
- I rarely stay at home during holidays.　节假日期间,我很少待在家里。
- I do...less often.　我不经常做……
- That is the last thing I will do in the world.　那是我决不会做的事情。

五、表示喜欢

- I particularly like / enjoy...　我特别喜欢……
- I have grown fond of sb. / sth. / doing sth.　我已经喜欢上某人 / 某物 / 做某事。
- Nobody loves...more than I do.　没有人比我更喜欢……
- Nothing gives me more pleasure than...　没有什么比……更能让我愉悦了。
- ...never fails to attract my attention.　……总是能吸引我的注意。

六、解释原因

- because / as...　因为……,由于……
- since / now that...　由于……,既然……
- in that　在于……
- thanks to...　由于……,多亏了……
- due to the fact that...　由于……
- because of　因为……

七、表示强调

- It was the teacher who helped me pass the exam.　正是这位老师帮助我通过了考试。
- It is this book that I read a lot.　我经常读的就是这本书。

- It was yesterday that I went to the museum. 我是昨天去的博物馆。
- It was at the museum that I met him yesterday. 我是昨天在博物馆遇见他的。
- It was not until the police came that I left. 直到警察来了我才走。
- Do sit down. 务必请坐。

八、There be 句型

- There is / are... 有……
- There was / there were... 过去有……
- There used to be... 过去曾有……
- There have / has been... 一直有……
- There seems / appears to be... 好像

有……
- There could be... 可能有……
- There should be... 应该会有……
- There must be... 一定有……

Notes

第二节 常用句法

一、定语从句

定语从句分为限定性定语从句和非限定性定语从句。限定性定语从句对先行词起修饰、限定作用，如果去掉限定性定语从句，句子意思会不完整。限定性定语从句的关系词包括：that、which、who、whom、whose、as 等。例如：

- The work that / which has just been finished is very important. 刚刚完成的那项工作非常重要。

- Do you know the reason why he is absent? 你知道他缺席的原因吗？

- I still remember the day when I first came to America. 我依然记得我第一次来美国的那一天。

非限定性定语从句用逗号与主句隔开，对主句起补充说明作用，不影响前面的句义，有时相当于一个并列分句或状语从句，可以表达原因、目的、结果、条件、让步等意义。非限定性定语从句的常用关系词包括：which、who、whom、whose、as 等。例如：

- He passed the interview, which was a pleasant surprise. (=He passed the interview, and it was a pleasant surprise.) 他通过了面试，这真是一个惊喜。

- This is London, which I have visited several times. 这就是伦敦，一个我已经来过数次的地方。

- He has been studying here for three months, during which he has made great progress. 他已经在这儿学习了三个月了，在这期间他取得了很大进步。

二、主语从句

在复合句中做主语的从句叫作主语从句。引导主语从句的连词主要包括：

从属连词：that、whether
连接代词：who、whom、whose、whoever、what、whatever、which、whichever
连接副词：why、when、whenever、where、wherever、how、however

- That he failed the exam surprised us all. 他考试没通过，这让我们十分惊讶。

- Whether we will go fishing this weekend remains undecided. 我们周末是否去钓鱼仍未决定。

- Whatever you do is not my concern.　你做的任何事都与我无关。
- What we need now is time.　我们现在需要的是时间。

为了防止句子头重脚轻，通常把形式主语 it 放在句首，而真正的主语置于句末。

- It is probable that he knows everything.　他可能什么都知道了。
- It is no surprise that the audience likes this performance.　观众们喜欢这场演出，这不奇怪。
- It is said that Jack has migrated to America.　据说杰克已经移民去了美国。

三、宾语从句

在主从复合句中充当宾语，位于及物动词、介词或复合谓语之后的从句称为宾语从句。宾语从句分为三类：动词的宾语从句、介词的宾语从句和形容词的宾语从句。

1. 动词的宾语从句

- I can't imagine how he did it.　我无法想象他是怎么做的。
- They couldn't understand why I refused it.　他们不能理解我为什么拒绝这件事。
- Do you know (that) he has joined the army?　你知道他已经参军了吗？

2. 介词的宾语从句

- It all depends on how we view the question.　这完全依赖于我们如何看待这个问题。
- We are worrying about what we should do next.　我们担心的是接下来应该做什么。
- I can judge by what I know of him.　我能通过我对他的了解来判断。

3. 形容词的宾语从句

- I am sorry I am late.　抱歉我迟到了。
- I am glad you are here.　我很高兴你在这儿。
- I'm afraid I can't go with you.　我恐怕不能跟你走。

四、表语从句

表语通常位于系动词之后，作用是说明主语的身份、性质、品性、特征和状态等。在复合句中做表语的从句叫作表语从句。常见的引导表语从句的连词有 when、where、why、who、how、that。

- My decision is that all of us are to start at 6 o'clock tomorrow morning.　我的决定是我们所有人明天早上六点开始。

- The problem is where we should go. 问题是我们应该去哪儿。
- These tools are not what we need. 这些工具不是我们所需要的。

五、同位语从句

同位语从句指在复合句中充当同位语的从句,用来对其前面的抽象名词进行解释说明。可以跟同位语从句的名词通常有 news、idea、fact、promise、question、doubt、thought、hope、message、suggestion、decision 等。引导同位语从句的词通常有连词 that、whether,连接代词 what、who,连接副词 how、when、where 等。注意 if 不能引导同位语从句。

- There is a feeling in me that we will meet one day. 我有一种感觉,总有一天我们会见面的。
- I heard the news that our class had won the game. 我听到了我们班赢了这场比赛的消息。
- He has to face the problem whether he will resign or not. 他必须面对他是否辞职的问题。

六、状语从句

状语从句指在句中起副词作用的句子,可以修饰谓语、非谓语动词、定语、状语或整个句子。状语从句根据其作用可分为时间、地点、原因、目的、结果、条件、让步、方式和比较等从句。

1. 时间状语从句

- When I studied there, I used to go to the library on Sundays. 我先前在那儿学习的时候,常在星期日去图书馆。
- Please don't talk loud while others are trying to focus. 当其他人试图集中注意力时,请不要大声说话。
- As time goes on, it is getting warmer and warmer. 随着时间的推移,天气越来越暖和。
- He remained there until / till the owner arrived. 他一直待在那里直到主人赶来。
- Not until you told me did I have any idea of it. 直到你告诉我我才知道这件事。
- She has been working in this factory since she left school. 她离开学校后一直在这家工厂工作。

2. 地点状语从句

- Generally, air will be heavily polluted where there are factories. 一般来说,有工厂的地方空气污染就严重。

- You are free to go wherever you are in mood for.　你可以自由地去任何你想去的地方。
- Where there is a will, there is a way.　有志者事竟成。

3. 原因状语从句

- I was absent from the meeting because I was busy preparing something more important.　我缺席会议是因为我正忙着准备更重要的事情。
- As it is raining, we shall not go to the picnic.　由于下雨，我们不去野餐了。
- Now that / since everybody is here, let's begin our party.　既然大家都来了，我们就开始我们的聚会吧。

4. 目的状语从句

- I will speak slowly so that you can catch my meaning.　我会说慢一点儿，好让你明白我的意思。
- In order that we might see the sunrise, we started for the peak early.　为了能看到日出，我们很早就出发去了山顶。
- Mary didn't want to go to the field trip for fear that she might waste too much time.　玛丽不想去实地考察，因为她怕会浪费太多时间。
- Take your raincoat in case it rains tomorrow.　带上你的雨衣以防明天下雨。

5. 结果状语从句

- Mike is such an interesting person that we all like talking with him.　迈克是一个非常有趣的人，我们都喜欢和他交谈。
- It was such lousy weather that we all failed to go to the park.　天气如此糟糕，我们都没能去成公园。
- He earned so much money that he could support his family.　他挣了这么多钱，足以养家糊口。

6. 条件状语从句

- You will fail the exam unless you study hard.　如果你不努力学习，考试就会不及格。
- As long as you follow the instruction, you will succeed.　只要你按照指示去做，你就会成功。
- Supposing (that) they refuse us, who else can we turn to for help?　假如他们拒绝我们，我们还能向谁求助呢？

7. 方式状语从句

- Do as you want, or you will regret.　你想怎么做就怎么做，否则你会后悔的。
- The teacher treats the students as if they were her own children.　这位老师对待学生就像对待自己的孩子一样。

8. 让步状语从句

- He is unhappy, though / although he has a lot of money.　尽管他很有钱，但是他不开心。
- Although / though it was raining hard, they went on the trip.　尽管雨下得很大，他们还是去旅行了。
- Even if I were busy, I would help you.　即便我很忙，我也会帮你。

9. 比较状语从句

- She is as pretty as her mother.　她和她妈妈一样漂亮。
- The house is three times as big as ours.　这房子是我们的房子的三倍大。
- The more you exercise, the healthier you will be.　你运动得越多，你就越健康。
- Oil is to machine what food is to men.　油之于机器，犹如食物于之人。

Notes